Fun and Fabulous
Patchwork & Appliqué

40 QUICK-TO-STITCH PROJECTS AND KEEPSAKES

GAIL LAWTHER

D&C

David and Charles

Contents

A DAVID & CHARLES BOOK
Copyright © David & Charles Limited 2007

David & Charles is an F+W Publications Inc. company
4700 East Galbraith Road
Cincinnati, OH 45236

First published in the UK in 2007

Text and designs copyright © Gail Lawther 2007
Photography and illustrations copyright © David & Charles 2007

Gail Lawther has asserted her right to be identified as
author of this work in accordance with the Copyright,
Designs and Patents Act, 1988.

ISBN: 978-0-7153-2324-3 hardback
ISBN: 978-0-7153-2481-3 paperback (USA only)

Printed in China by SNP Lee Fung
for David & Charles
Brunel House   Newton Abbot   Devon

Executive Editor Cheryl Brown
Editors Ame Verso and Jennifer Fox-Proverbs
Project Editor Lin Clements
Art Editor Prudence Rogers
Designer Jodie Lystor
Photographers Karl Adamson and Kim Sayer
Production Controller Ros Napper

Visit our website at www.davidandcharles.co.uk

David & Charles books are available from all good bookshops; alternatively
you can contact our Orderline on 0870 9908222 or write to us at FREEPOST
EX2 110, D&C Direct, Newton Abbot, TQ12 4ZZ (no stamp required UK only);
US customers call 800-289-0963 and Canadian customers call 800-840-5220.

Introduction

Patchwork and quilting is a deeply satisfying craft – every stage is enjoyable. Each project starts from a tiny seed of an idea: could I…? Would it work if…? Then there's the refining: creating your own design or picking just the right one from a book or magazine. Next comes the fun of choosing the fabrics, followed by the soothing processes of piecing or appliqué – and finally the quilting and finishing. Any large quilt is a labour of love, and once it's finished it produces an enormous sense of achievement. But you can't rush it.

Sometimes, though, you simply want to work on something that comes together more quickly – a beautiful finished item that shows off your skills and love of fabric, without taking a significant chunk of your life! That's exactly why I've created the projects in this book. Each one is small but will give you that same buzz of achievement and satisfaction without taking too long to create. I've called them patchwork and appliqué keepsakes, as they are all fun things that the owner will treasure. Most of them have been inspired by the many celebrations that take place throughout our lives, and any of the projects would make a perfect gift, either as a gesture of friendship or to celebrate some special occasion. Or why not stitch some of them just for yourself?

Whatever patchwork techniques you enjoy, you'll find something that appeals among the projects in this book. Each technique is explained within the project, so if you'd like to try Italian corded quilting, or felt appliqué, you'll find all the information you need. You'll also find that each project has an easiness rating (from one star through to five), so you can pick one to suit your confidence level.

Throughout the book you will see that I've made lavish use of some of the wonderful embellishments available: these buttons, beads, charms, ribbons, braids and specialist threads make the finished items irresistible. Several of the projects are also embellished with hand embroidery, but don't worry if this is a new skill to you – at the back of the book you'll find instructions for all the stitches I've used, along with a few extra ones for your own variations.

And, speaking of variations, each project also includes an alternative idea – a suggestion for varying the colourway, or a complementary design using the same technique, or the same design embellished in a different way. And, of course, I'm hoping that you'll add your own ideas to mine, creating still more variations of the basic projects. Flip through the pages, and you'll find that you can't wait to get started!

Fabrics

You're probably expecting me to say that for patchwork you should only work in 100% cotton fabrics. Well, I'm not going to say it! Certainly cottons are the best for traditional patchwork projects that might need laundering – for instance, the Christmas breadcloth on page 111 – but for many of these keepsake pieces laundering won't be a consideration, so your choice of fabrics is much wider.

Cottons

Let's begin with the cottons first of all. If you visit any fabric store (either in person or on the internet), you will find a wonderful array of cotton fabrics on offer. Single-coloured (plain or solid) fabrics are available in every conceivable colour, while mottled or marbled fabrics give a similar impression to plains but have a little more visual interest. Tie-dyed and random-dyed cottons can produce some lovely serendipitous effects in the finished work; I used a random-dyed cotton fabric for the Locket Pocket on page 39. Batiks are very popular and are often very tightly woven, which makes them excellent for any technique that requires sharp creases, for instance the folded star patchwork on page 14, or the quick Prairie Points on page 63. The tight weave can make these fabrics quite hard

work, though, if you plan to sew by hand; if you're not sure, try a little piece out with your chosen method before you make the final choice for your project.

Print fabrics can range from tiny, almost invisible overall prints through to large, bold patterns. As a general rule, keep large prints for quite large patches, so that the printed pattern doesn't overwhelm the lines of your design. Many cotton fabrics are overprinted with a metallic design, which again can be subtle or bold.

Some cottons are printed or woven with stripes or checks; these can be a bit difficult to use, as the visual effect of the fabrics is very strong, but if they're incorporated well they can be very effective. I've been able to make good use of a checked fabric for the teddy's tablecloth on page 13.

Silks

Many people are wary of using silk in patchwork, but if you choose the right kind it's very easy to work with and produces the most beautiful effects as the surface sheen catches the light. Use a good-quality silk dupion rather than any other kind of silk fabric, as dupion is fairly firmly woven and takes a good, crisp crease, which is useful for folded techniques. Silk frays more than cotton fabric, so if you're piecing with it, cut a larger seam allowance than usual to make it easier to work with. Dupion makes a suitably opulent background for the album cover designs to celebrate special anniversaries (see pages 93 and 95), the ring cushion (page 29), and the special occasion photograph frames (pages 49 and 51).

Metallics

I often use metallic fabrics in my work, particularly as I do a lot of decorative stained-glass patchwork. Modern metallic fabrics are very good-natured; some of them can be pressed and pieced in exactly the same way as cottons, but some of them can tend to catch on the iron – particularly any fabric with a sequinned surface. If you're thinking of using a particular metallic fabric for your work, test a piece first of all to see how it behaves. Try a tiny corner with a point of the iron; if it tends to stick, press it from the back, or use a non-stick sheet between the fabric and the iron. A woven metallic/synthetic brocade makes a perfect centrepiece for the album cover on page 93.

Synthetics

The variety of synthetic fabrics available is enormous, including woven Lurex fabrics, plasticized surfaces and imitation silks and satins. They can work very well as 'sparkle' fabrics – unusual choices that add a little surprise to a conventional design. Like the metallics, they vary enormously in the way they behave when they're pressed, stitched or quilted, so try a sample piece first.

Sheers

Sheer fabrics and laces make pretty additions to some of these keepsake projects and I've used a shot gauze and a metallic mesh for the herb sachets on pages 87 and 90. Lace works well on the windows of the new home picture (see page 75) and the 1930s swimming costume design (see page 43), and I've used motifs cut from guipure lace to create the appliqué design on the ring cushion (see page 29).

Felts

Felt has come a long way from the chunky fabrics we cut up for school projects; it's now available in all kinds of wonderful colours and finishes, including random-dyed and metallic effects. Felt is a thick fabric, so it's not suitable for traditional piecing, but it's just right for quirky designs such as the needlebook and pincushion on page 21. No seams are needed because felt doesn't fray.

Threads & Embellishments

After drooling over all the fabrics available today, there comes the enjoyable task of selecting threads and embellishments to bring your patchwork to life. The projects in this book give you plenty of examples of yummy items you can use.

Threads

The threads I've used on these keepsakes really fall into two main categories – practical and decorative. Practical threads comprise ordinary hand-sewing and machine-sewing threads, which are used for assembling the projects whether you're stitching by hand or machine.

For tasks that require strong thread, such as stitching together the two parts of the photograph frame (page 49) or the bridal handbag (page 69), you'll find buttonhole thread or quilting thread useful.

Decorative threads are infinite in their colour, variety and finish; they include stranded embroidery cotton (floss), soft cotton, coton perlé, coton à broder, and metallic threads for hand or machine. Variegated threads have become very popular in the past few years – most of the types mentioned above are available in variegated versions.

You may wish to decorate your versions of these projects with more quilting and there are special quilting threads produced for both hand quilting and machine quilting and these threads are often a little stronger than regular threads.

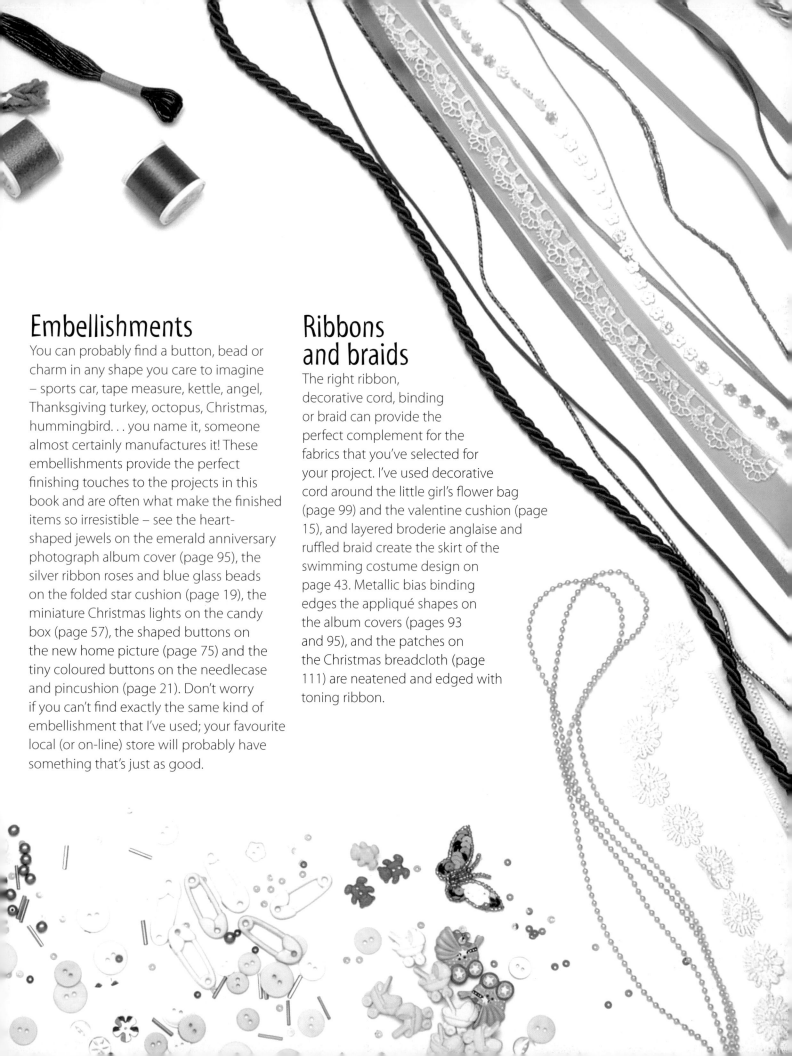

Embellishments

You can probably find a button, bead or charm in any shape you care to imagine – sports car, tape measure, kettle, angel, Thanksgiving turkey, octopus, Christmas, hummingbird. . . you name it, someone almost certainly manufactures it! These embellishments provide the perfect finishing touches to the projects in this book and are often what make the finished items so irresistible – see the heart-shaped jewels on the emerald anniversary photograph album cover (page 95), the silver ribbon roses and blue glass beads on the folded star cushion (page 19), the miniature Christmas lights on the candy box (page 57), the shaped buttons on the new home picture (page 75) and the tiny coloured buttons on the needlecase and pincushion (page 21). Don't worry if you can't find exactly the same kind of embellishment that I've used; your favourite local (or on-line) store will probably have something that's just as good.

Ribbons and braids

The right ribbon, decorative cord, binding or braid can provide the perfect complement for the fabrics that you've selected for your project. I've used decorative cord around the little girl's flower bag (page 99) and the valentine cushion (page 15), and layered broderie anglaise and ruffled braid create the skirt of the swimming costume design on page 43. Metallic bias binding edges the appliqué shapes on the album covers (pages 93 and 95), and the patches on the Christmas breadcloth (page 111) are neatened and edged with toning ribbon.

Welcome to the World

Greet a new baby with this delightful handmade card, where a cute sleepsuit hangs from its own little washing line, complete with miniature wooden pegs (clothes pins). The motif is created in machine cutwork and the raw edges of the fabric patches are sealed and embellished with machine satin stitch. Once the motif is stitched, you can add little button or charm details – or even stitch the baby's initials on to the sleepsuit. If teddy bears are your thing, try the sweet card on page 13.

Easiness Rating ✳✳
Techniques Used Machine cutwork/satin stitch • Fraying
Finished Size Design fits on a card blank 13 x 20cm (5 x 8in)

You will need...

- ✓ 13cm (5in) square of print fabric for the sleepsuit
- ✓ 6 x 4cm (2½ x 1½in) pale denim fabric for collar
- ✓ 6 x 4cm (2½ x 1½in) double-sided bonding web
- ✓ 13cm (5in) square of Stitch 'n' Tear or similar foundation fabric
- ✓ 13cm (5in) square compressed wadding (batting)
- ✓ 11.5 x 18cm (4½ x 7in) loosely woven pastel plaid fabric
- ✓ Four tiny buttons or round beads and one tiny heart button or charm
- ✓ Threads to match the buttons/beads
- ✓ 10cm (4in) length of fine white cord
- ✓ Two miniature pegs (clothes pins)
- ✓ Sewing thread to match or contrast with the sleepsuit fabrics
- ✓ Single-fold card blank 13 x 20cm (5 x 8in)
- ✓ Stick glue
- ✓ Soft pencil

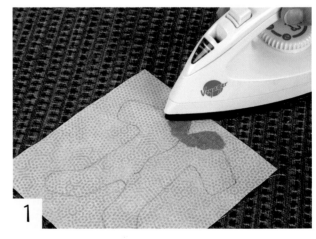

Using the template on page 13, trace the two sides of the collar on to the paper (smooth) side of the bonding web. Lay the bonding web glue (rough) side down on the back of the denim fabric and fuse into place with a warm iron. Cut out the collar pieces. Use a soft pencil to trace the outline of the sleepsuit on to the right side of the print fabric; remove the paper from the bonding web and fuse the collar pieces into position on the sleepsuit shape. ➤

2

Lay the print fabric right side up on the square of wadding (batting) and work a small machine zigzag all round the outline of the design. Using small, sharp-pointed scissors, cut the shape out just beyond the line of zigzag.

Lay the sleepsuit shape on the square of Stitch 'n' Tear and set your machine to a medium-width satin stitch. Stitch all round the edge of the shape in a toning colour, then stitch down the line marking the front opening, tapering the line of stitching at the bottom. In a different thread colour, stitch round the edges of the collar pieces.

3

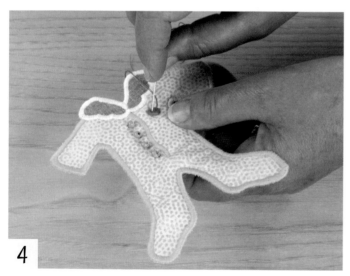

4

Pull the Stitch 'n' Tear away from the edges of the design and then embellish the sleepsuit with the little buttons/beads and the heart motif or charm.

Smart Stitch

If you can't track down Stitch 'n' Tear, use a piece of white cartridge paper as a foundation instead.

Fray the edges of the woven plaid fabric to a depth of roughly 1.25cm (½in) all round, and stick it to the front of the card to create a background. Tie a knot in each end of the cord and stitch or stick the cord on to the woven background. Peg the sleepsuit on to the washing line to complete your card.

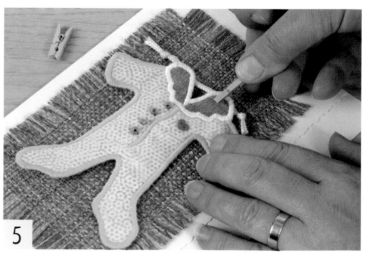

5

Teddy Bear's Picnic

Any teddy bear would find this picnic irresistible! Use the template below to create the shape from mottled brown fabric, neatening the edges as described for the main project. Embroider on the nose, mouth and ear details, and then add little beads for the eyes and buttons. Use pinking shears to cut rectangles of 'sky' and 'grass' fabrics and stick them to the front of the card, then fray a square of plaid fabric for the blanket and fold it into a triangle. Stick the blanket shape to the grass and add the bear shape. Embellish with yummy picnic items.

Teddy Bear template (full size)
*Trace the bear design on to the right side
of mottled brown fabric*

Sleepsuit template (full size)
*Trace the collar template on to the paper
side of the bonding web, and then trace
the complete design on to the right side
of your print fabric*

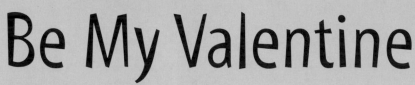

Be My Valentine

Rich red and gold print fabrics create a sumptuous pillow for Valentine's Day, embellished with heart details and twisted cords in toning colours. The central design is made from folded Prairie Points, built up in circuits to create a star design. If you use lots of different print fabrics that feature hearts, your valentine is sure to get the message. For a sweet-scented pillow add some pot-pourri as you stuff the shape or some dried herbs or lavender. For a different mood, try the midnight blue and silver version on page 18.

Easiness Rating ✳✳✳
Techniques Used Prairie Points • Folded star patchwork • Twisted cord
Finished Size 23cm (9in) square

You will need...

✓ Two 25cm (10in) squares of heart-print cotton fabric

✓ 7.5cm (3in) squares of four different toning print fabrics: four of fabric A and eight each of fabrics B, C and D

✓ 51cm (20in) gold fusible bias binding, 6mm (¼in) wide

✓ 20cm (8in) square of firm white or cream foundation fabric

✓ Heart-shaped motifs or beads for embellishment, plus matching threads

✓ Golden-yellow sewing thread

✓ Synthetic stuffing and a small amount of pot-pourri

✓ 20cm (8in) square of plain paper

✓ 1.25m (1½yd) of twisted cord, bought or home-made

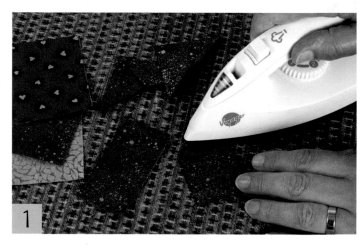

To create a Prairie Point, fold one of the 7.5cm (3in) fabric squares in half, right side out, and press. Fold each short edge of the rectangle diagonally to create a point. Do this with each of the small squares of print fabric. ➤

2

Use a ruler and soft pencil to draw the diagonals across the square of foundation fabric, and then draw in the horizontal and vertical halfway lines. These lines will help you to position the Prairie Points to create an accurate star design. Position the four Prairie Points you have created from fabric A in the centre of the foundation square, so that the points meet in the centre and the edges are aligned with the marked diagonals. Pin the patches in place, then go round the raw edges with a medium-width machine zigzag.

3

Pin four Prairie Points made from fabric B on top of the first four, positioning them so that their points are a scant 2cm (¾in) out from the centre of the design. Then pin the remaining four fabric B patches on top to create a star design. Machine this circuit of patches in place. Add a circuit of Prairie Points made from fabric C – don't worry about the little gaps between the patches as these will be covered by the final circuit of points.

4

Add the final circuit of Prairie Points made from fabric D and stitch them in place.

5

Trace the circle from page 18 on to paper and cut it out. Lay the circle centrally over the star design and check that all the stitching is outside the circle. If not, cut the circle down slightly until all the stitching is revealed. Once your circle is the correct size, trace it on to the centre of one square of print fabric and cut away the central circle to create a border for the star design.

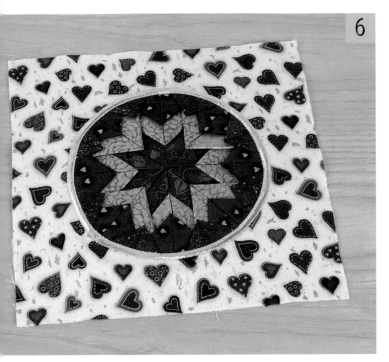

6

Pin the fabric square over the star design and stitch it in place with machine zigzag. Cover the line of zigzag with a line of fusible bias binding, folding under the raw ends to create a smooth circle, and then stitch the binding in place by hand or machine.

7

Put the star design and remaining square of print fabric right sides together, aligning raw edges. Stitch a 1.25cm (½in) seam all around the edges, leaving 10cm (4in) open for turning. Clip corners and turn out. Embellish with heart-shaped motifs or beads, then stuff the cushion gently with a mixture of stuffing and pot-pourri.

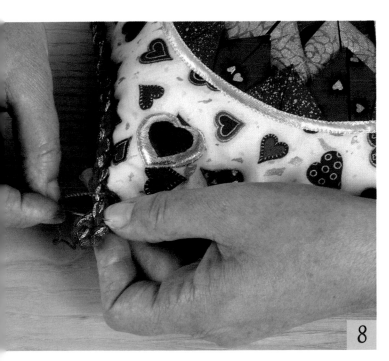

8

Slipstitch the opening closed and then trim the edges of the pillow with twisted cord (see page 101). Begin the line of cord at one corner of the pillow, and add a loop at each corner for extra interest. The ends of the cord can be hidden under the final loop.

Smart Stitch

Just stuff the pillow gently; if you fill it too full, the points of the star design will stick up rather than lying flat.

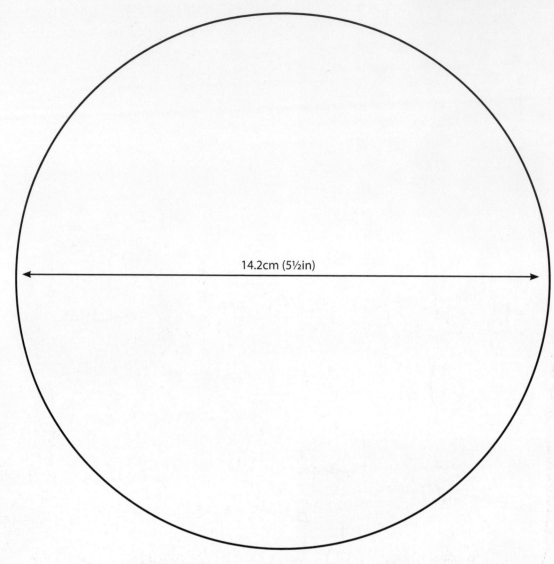

Be My Valentine template (full size)
Trace this circle and cut it out; check the size on the star design before using it as a template for cutting your print fabric border

14.2cm (5½in)

Midnight Star

For a completely different effect, make your star from Prairie Points in midnight blue and silver prints, set off by one circuit of white lamé patches. A circle of silver bias binding complements the print fabrics, and I've used padded silver heart motifs topped with silver ribbon roses to embellish the finished pillow.

Funky Felt

The San Blas Islands in central America are famous for exquisite mola work stitched by Cuna Indians. These molas, or cloths, are used as garments and feature stylized animal and bird motifs worked in many layers of brightly coloured fabrics. The Cuna use a complex method of reverse appliqué, but here I've used a simpler technique for this mola-style butterfly needlebook; the beaky bird pincushion is even easier. Because the layers are in felt, there is no need to turn the edges under to neaten them.

Easiness Rating ✳✳✳
Techniques Used Hand appliqué • Hand embroidery
Finished Size Needlecase 13.5cm (5½in) square; pincushion 12.5cm (5in) square

Beaky Bird

A quirky bird decorates this colourful pincushion, which makes a perfect partner for the needlebook. Use two 12.5cm (5in) squares of felt, the template on page 23 and the same technique as the main project to build up the design on the front piece, embellishing it with beads, tiny buttons and random cross stitches. To make the spiral on the wings easier to work with, secure it at each end with a button first, then add one in the middle and fill in the gaps with more buttons. Join the octagons with a line of running stitches, adding some polyester stuffing between the shapes before you finish joining them.

You will need...

- ✓ Four 13.5cm (5½in) squares of felt in different colours for the 'pages' of the needlebook
- ✓ Large and small scraps of felt in assorted bright colours for the appliqué; the main wings piece needs to be at least 12.5cm (5in) square
- ✓ Cotons à broder in various bright colours
- ✓ Assorted tiny buttons and small beads in bright colours

Trace or photocopy the butterfly design overleaf and cut it out around the octagon. Use this shape as a template for trimming off the corners of the four large felt squares. ➤

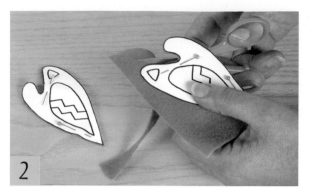

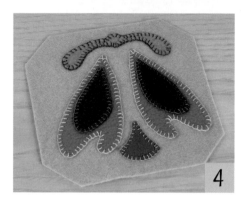

3

Choose one of the four octagons to be the cover of the needlebook and pin the main wing shapes on to it – make sure that you leave space for the other parts of the design, particularly the head sections. Work blanket stitch (see page 116) around the edges of the patches, using coton à broder in a contrasting colour.

Cut out the main wing shapes and use these as templates for cutting two shapes from the appropriate felt.

Smart Stitch

Don't try and work blanket stitch around the tiny patches of the design; it's much easier – and quicker – to secure them with beads or buttons.

4

Cut the large head shape, the tail and the inner wings from the paper pattern, and use these as templates to cut felt patches in different colours. Add these to the design, again using blanket stitch in contrasting colours for the appliqué.

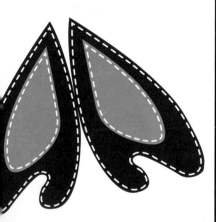

Butterfly template (full size)
Trace or photocopy this design and cut it out around the octagon. Use the octagon shape as a guide for cutting the four 'leaves' of the needlebook, then cut up the pattern in stages to produce templates for the other felt patches

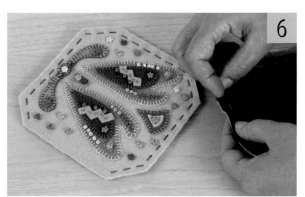

5 Cut the zigzag shape on the wings out of the paper pattern and use this template to cut the two shapes from felt. Secure them on the wings with a few straight stitches in a contrasting colour. Cut the small felt shapes for the ends of the antennae, the extra patch under the head and the centre of the tail out of felt. Add these to the design in the appropriate places, securing them with some tiny coloured buttons. Now embellish the design with small beads, and embroider the bottom of each wing with a curved line of fern stitch (see page 117).

6 Stitch the four 'pages' together in pairs with a large running stitch (see page 118) in a contrasting colour for each pair. Leave the left side of the butterfly design, and one long edge of the other octagon, unstitched.

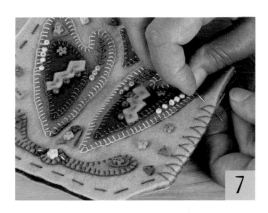

Lay the pairs together, trimming the shapes slightly if necessary so that they match perfectly, and use a contrasting thread to stitch a line of large closed buttonhole stitches (see blanket stitch page 116) down the spine of the book. Make the gaps between the spacing stitches very short, so that the triangles made by the closed stitches almost meet at the base.

Beaky Bird template (full size)
Trace or photocopy this design and cut it out around the octagon. Use the octagon shape as a guide for cutting the front and back of the pincushion, then cut up the pattern in stages to produce templates for the other felt patches

Star of Wonder

Bring a beautiful sparkle to your festive decorations with these lovely Christmas decorations. They are made using a variation of English patchwork: the fabric patches are secured over thin card shapes, which then stay in the designs to stiffen them. Once the decorations have been stitched you will have great fun embellishing them with all kinds of beads, braids, jewels and sequins.

Easiness Rating ✳✳✳
Techniques Used English patchwork over card
Finished Size 19 x 15cm (7½ x 6in)

You will need...

for one decoration

- ✓ 20 x 15cm (8 x 6in) fabric for the arms of the star
- ✓ 15 x 11cm (6 x 4½in) fabric for the top point of the star
- ✓ 18 x 13cm (7 x 5in) fabric for the bottom point of the star
- ✓ 25 x 15cm (10 x 6in) thin card
- ✓ Glue stick
- ✓ Sewing thread to blend with your fabrics
- ✓ Toning beads, jewels, charms, sequins or other decorations
- ✓ 20cm (8in) fine decorative cord for hanging loop

You will be making a double-sided star, with two pieced shapes sewn together. Trace or photocopy the templates A–D overleaf; stick the shapes on to thin card, then cut them out. Use templates A and B as guides to cut shapes from card; for each decoration you will need six of shape A and two of shape B. Now use templates C and D as guides to cut patches from the fabrics: the fabric patches will be 6mm (¼in) larger all round than their matching card shapes. For each decoration you will need six patches of shape C (four in one fabric for the arms of the star and two in a different fabric for the top point), and two patches of shape D. ➤

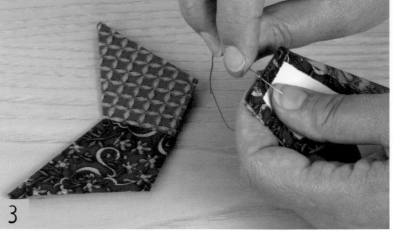

Lay each fabric patch right side down and carefully position the matching card template on top so there is an even border of fabric all the way around. Fold the excess fabric over the card template and secure in place with a small amount of stick glue.

Place two A shapes in different fabrics right sides together, and join the pair by oversewing along one edge – check the orientation of the shapes carefully to make sure that you're joining the correct edges. Now join an A shape and a B shape as shown, once again checking their orientation. Join the pairs to create a star shape, then make a second star shape in the same way.

Star of Wonder templates (full size)
Use template A to cut six shapes from card,
and template B to cut two shapes from card.
Use template C to cut six fabric patches,
and template D to cut two fabric patches

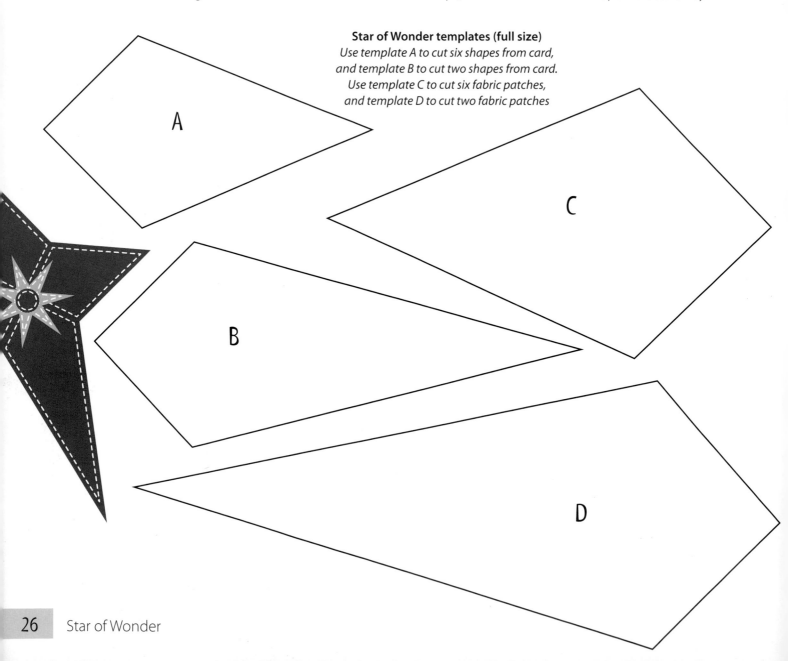

A

C

B

D

4

Place the two stars card sides together and join them by oversewing around all the edges. As you work around the shape, add beads at the ends of the side points, and sandwich the raw ends of the hanging loop between the card shapes at the top point.

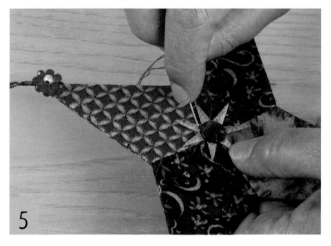

5

Once the star shapes are joined, stitch a string of extra beads to the bottom of the star, and stitch any extra embellishments to the centre front.

Stellar Jewel

This star ornament is made in the same way as the main project but uses only one diamond shape. Use templates E and F, below, cutting twelve of E from card and twelve of F from fabric. I used green and gold prints cut from a lovely silk sari brocade. Embellish with jewels, beads and braid as desired.

Smart Stitch

Don't worry about the fabric sticking out slightly from the narrow point of each shape; you can neaten the excess by trimming or tucking it in as you stitch the shapes together.

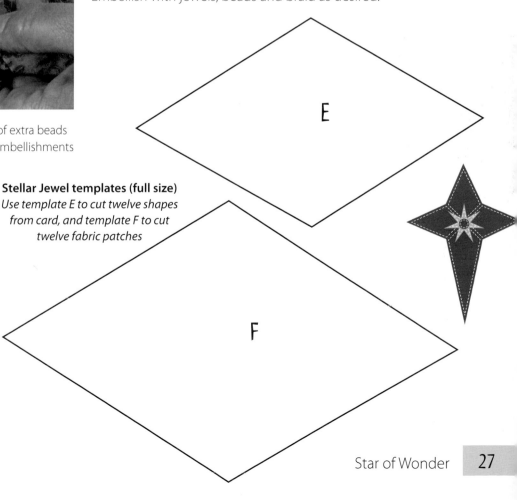

Stellar Jewel templates (full size)
Use template E to cut twelve shapes from card, and template F to cut twelve fabric patches

E

F

Together Forever

Display your wedding rings on the special day on this pretty cushion; if you tie them on securely, even the smallest pageboy or flower girl can keep them safe during the walk up the aisle! The quilted design is decorated with appliquéd guipure lace motifs, in a mix of large and small motifs to make it easier to fill the heart shape.

Easiness Rating ✳✳✳
Techniques Used Lace appliqué • Machine quilting
Finished Size 25cm (10in) square

You will need...

✓ Two 25cm (10in) squares of white or ivory silk dupion

✓ 115cm (45in) bias strip of matching silk dupion, 3.5cm (1½in) wide

✓ Two 25cm (10in) squares of compressed wadding (batting)

✓ Small amount of polyester stuffing

✓ White sewing thread

✓ Assorted motifs cut from guipure lace

✓ Small white pearl beads and four small pearly-white heart buttons

✓ 30cm (12in) lengths of thin pink and blue ribbon

✓ Sewing threads to match the ribbons

✓ Fading pen

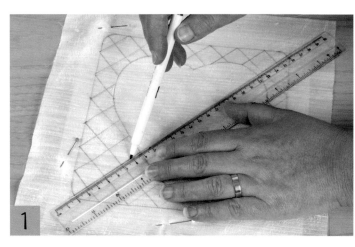

Occasionally fading pens can leave permanent marks on silk dupion, so practise on a fabric scrap first. If the marks have not faded completely after 24 hours, use a chalk marker, alabaster pencil or a silverpoint to trace the design. Trace or photocopy the template on page 32. Lay one square of dupion over the design so that there is an even border of fabric all the way around the design. Pin the layers together and then use your chosen marker to trace all the lines of the design. Remove the pins. ➤

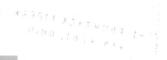

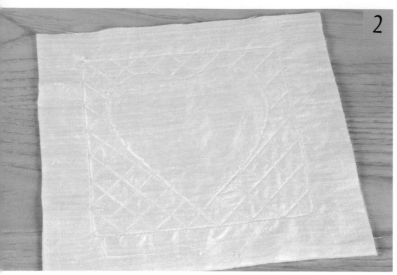

2 Pin the marked design on to one of the squares of wadding, right side up, and stitch by machine along all the marked lines. If you have a walking foot on your machine you may find it useful for this stage; a walking foot helps to prevent quilted designs from puckering as they feed through under the machine foot.

Arrange the lace motifs inside the heart shape so that they fill it out evenly. When you're happy with the arrangement, pin them in place and appliqué the motifs with small hand stitches.

3

4

Smart Stitch

Add the beads at this stage, rather than earlier, so that your sewing thread doesn't catch on them when you're doing the applique.

Lay the spare square of silk dupion on a flat surface and cover it with the remaining square of wadding. Put a little polyester stuffing in the centre of the wadding to pad the centre of the cushion and then put the appliqué design on top, right side up. Pin the layers together and round the corners, and then begin pinning the binding in position on the front of the cushion, matching the raw edges. Fold the raw end under at the beginning of the line of binding and ease the binding round the curved corners of the cushion.

5 Machine around the edge of the binding, stitching roughly 6mm (¼in) in from the raw edges.

6

Turn the binding to the back of the cushion, fold under the raw edge and slipstitch it in place.

7 Stitch a little pearl at each intersection of the quilted design, and a pearly heart in each corner, as shown.

8 Fold each strip of ribbon in half and finger-press, then stitch one ribbon to each side of the quilted design, stitching through the fold. Trim the ends of the ribbons diagonally, and your ring cushion is all ready for the big day.

Together Forever template (full size)
Trace or photocopy the template, then use a fading pen (or other temporary marker) to trace the design on to one square of silk

Sweet Treats

Tiny bags of sweetmeats make lovely mementoes for wedding guests. Make the gorgeous little bags, shown here, out of rectangles of gold-printed sheer fabric and decorate them with individual guipure lace motifs. Fill each bag with confectionery, and then tie the tops with short lengths of ribbon or beading.

Under and Over

Ribbon weaving is given a new twist with this simple but striking table mat where the strips are stitched tubes of fabric embellished with braids. I used a selection of fabrics in rich colours from a single range, which creates a sense of unity across the design, but you could use totally different fabrics for a more random effect – see the cream lace version on page 37. These mats are so easy to make, you could stitch a whole set; a larger one in Christmas fabrics would look wonderful as a seasonal centrepiece.

Easiness Rating ✳
Techniques Used Fabric weaving • Simple machine appliqué
Finished Size 30cm (12in) square

You will need...

✓ 9 x 30cm (3½ x 12in) strips of cotton fabric, two each of eight different colours

✓ Four 6.5 x 38cm (2½ x 15in) strips of fabric for binding the edges (use some of the same fabrics as for the weaving, or choose contrasting fabric)

✓ 30cm (12in) strips of braid, lace and broderie anglaise to complement your fabrics

✓ Sewing thread in a neutral colour

Smart Stitch

If you're making several table mats you could use a rouleau turner to help you speed up the process of turning out the stitched tubes.

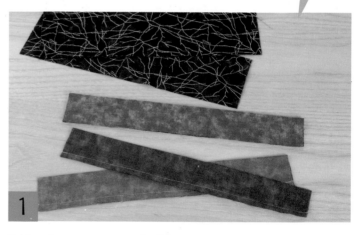

Fold each weaving strip in half down its length, right sides together, and stitch a 6mm (¼in) seam.

Turn each stitched tube right side out and press it into a flat strip, making sure that the seam is hidden at the back of the strip. ➤

Decorate some of the strips with braid, lace and so on, appliquéing the decoration by machine. Divide the strips into two piles of eight, distributing the decorated strips evenly between the piles, and trying different layouts to see which strips work best next to each other.

3

Once you've decided on the order of the strips, begin weaving the decorated strips in a simple under-and-over pattern. Work on a flat surface and, starting at one corner, add horizontal and vertical strips alternately, pinning the strips together as you go to secure them.

4

Once the woven design is complete, pull the strips together firmly so that they lie snugly against each other and pin. This should leave the raw ends of the strips overlapping the weaving by about 6mm (¼in) along each edge of the square. Go round the edge of the square with a large machine zigzag to secure the woven design and then remove the pins.

5

6

Bind opposite sides of the square with strips of binding fabric. Machine the strips to the front of the design, stitching just at the edge of the woven pattern. Trim the edges of the strip to the width of the mat and then fold the binding strip over the raw edges and slipstitch it to the back of the mat. To finish your mat, bind the remaining two sides in the same way, folding in the edges of each binding strip before you stitch so that it exactly fits the width of the mat.

Café au Lait

For the variation shown right, I made the mat in exactly the same way but used a colour scheme of cream and beige cotton fabrics, decorated with cream lace, braid and ricrac. For binding the mat I picked out one of the plainer fabrics from the woven design and used it for all the binding strips.

Locket Pocket

This padded pocket is ideal for storing spare jewellery when travelling, as it is small enough to slip into a handbag. The Log Cabin design is a traditional patchwork block, but to make it easy I've used foundation piecing, which ensures crisp, even patches without lots of measuring. I used a beautiful, random-dyed cotton that creates an intriguing secondary pattern when cut up and reassembled, but you could make it in silk dupion or metallics for extra glitz (see page 41).

Easiness Rating ✳✳
Techniques Used Foundation piecing • Simple hand embroidery
Finished Size 13.5cm (5½in) square

You will need...

- ✓ 15cm (6in) square of Stitch 'n' Tear or firm stitch-in interfacing
- ✓ 15cm (6in) square of 2oz polyester wadding (batting)
- ✓ 15cm (6in) square of compressed polyester wadding (batting)
- ✓ 36cm (14in) square of random-dyed fabric
- ✓ Two 10 x 15cm (4 x 6in) rectangles of backing fabric
- ✓ Sewing thread to tone with the fabrics
- ✓ Variegated coton perlé or silk thread in toning colours
- ✓ Beads to complement your colour scheme
- ✓ Rotary cutter, board and long ruler (optional)

1 Trace or photocopy the template overleaf and then use a soft pencil to trace it on to the square of interfacing. Write in the numbers.

2 Cut a 5cm (2in) square from the random-dyed fabric, and cut the rest of this fabric into 3cm (1¼in) strips. This gives more strips than you need, enabling you to pick just the section you want for each part of the design. Follow the foundation-piecing instructions in the panel on page 41 to create a Log Cabin block. ➤

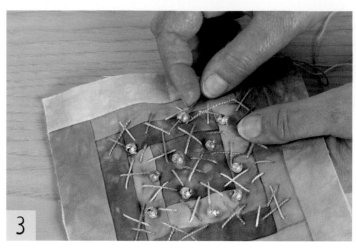

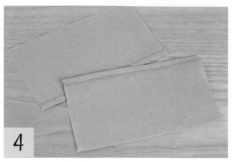

4

Press under and stitch a small double hem on one long side of each backing rectangle.

3

Pin the Log Cabin design right side up on to the square of compressed wadding (batting) and then embellish the central part of the block with overlapping long, straight stitches at random angles. Keep the embroidery away from the final circuit of patches, so that it won't be trapped in the seams. Once the embroidery is complete, add some beads around the central square.

Smart Stitch

If you don't have a rotary cutter and cutting board, draw the small square and the strips on to the fabric with a pencil and ruler and then cut along the lines with sharp scissors.

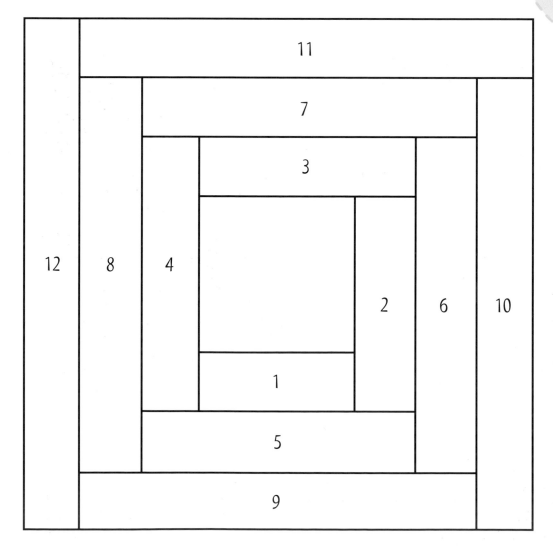

| 11 |
| 7 |
| 3 |

| 12 | 8 | 4 | | 2 | 6 | 10 |

| 1 |
| 5 |
| 9 |

Log Cabin template (full size)
Trace or photocopy the Log Cabin block design and draw it on to the square of interfacing

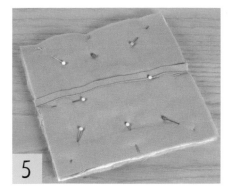

5

Lay the wadding square on a flat surface and cover it with the decorated square, right side up. Position the backing pieces on top, right sides down, overlapping them so the raw edges match all the way around. Pin all the layers together.

6

Stitch a 6mm (¼in) seam all the way around the square. Clip the corners and trim the wadding back to the seam line. Turn the pocket right way out and press just the very edges to set the seams.

In a nutshell...

Foundation piecing

Foundation piecing is stitched from the back of the work and at first this can seem slightly strange, but you will quickly get the hang of it. The technique allows you to create accurate patches on the front of the block, with perfect straight lines and square corners. If you design your own foundation-pieced design, remember to flip it right-to-left before tracing, as you will be working on it in reverse.

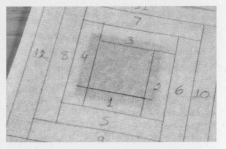

1 Use a pencil to trace the foundation-piecing design on to firm interfacing, using a ruler to keep straight lines accurate. Mark in the numbers. You will be stitching on the traced side of the interfacing but remember that this is the *back* of the block. Pin the cut square of fabric on to the other side of the interfacing, right side up, so that the edges overlap the drawn square evenly.

2 Choose a section of one of the cut fabric strips and cut a length to match one edge of the square. Pin this to the front of the work along the edge marked 1, right side down over the square patch, matching the raw edges. On the back, machine stitch along the edge of patch 1, extending the stitching a little each end.

3 Press the patch open from the front.

4 Cut a length of fabric to fit the edge of patch 2. Stitch it on and press as before.

5 Continue with patches 3 and 4 to complete the first circuit of patches.

6 Carry on adding patches until you have completed the block design.

Evening Stars

The same foundation-pieced design looks completely different if you stitch it in peacock-coloured silks. For this version I kept to the traditional Log Cabin layout of two sides light and two sides dark. I embroidered each strip with a machine stitch in gold thread and then decorated the centre patch with fake jewels and gold beads.

Dear Diary...

Wouldn't it be lovely to have your own personal postcard of each summer holiday? Why not make a journal to jot down all those little day-to-day details that make a holiday special? Decorate a bought notebook with a design that recalls a bygone era – the heyday of the seaside. The design is created from cut-out fabric shapes; once you have assembled the main patches of the design, you can embellish it with lace, cord and beach-themed buttons or beads. As an alternative, try the peaceful sailboat scene on page 45.

Easiness Rating ✳✳
Techniques Used Using fusible interfacing
Finished Size The design is 20 x 14cm (8 x 5½in)

You will need...

- ✓ Large scraps of three different 'sand' fabrics – the largest at least 15 x 5cm (6 x 2in)
- ✓ 15 x 7.5cm (6 x 3in) blue-green 'sea' fabric
- ✓ 15 x 10cm (6 x 4in) 'sky' fabric
- ✓ Scraps of cotton fabric in assorted prints and plains for the swimsuit (I used a red, white and blue colour scheme)
- ✓ 30cm (12in) square of iron-on interfacing
- ✓ 9cm (3½in) length of frilled ribbon, braid or broderie anglaise for the swimsuit skirt
- ✓ Small scraps of lace, cord, ricrac and braid for decoration
- ✓ Stick or fabric glue
- ✓ Charms, beads and buttons on a seaside theme, plus matching threads (or strong glue)
- ✓ Notebook with a cover at least 20 x 14cm (8 x 5½in)

1

Trace or photocopy the five background templates on page 46 and cut them out. Decide which of your fabrics you are going to use for which part of the background design and cut a piece of interfacing comfortably bigger than each template. Use a warm iron to fuse these pieces on to the backs of the relevant fabrics. ➤

2

Use the templates as guides to cut the shapes out of the stiffened fabrics, making sure that you position each template right side up on the right side of the fabric, so that the cut shapes are the right way round.

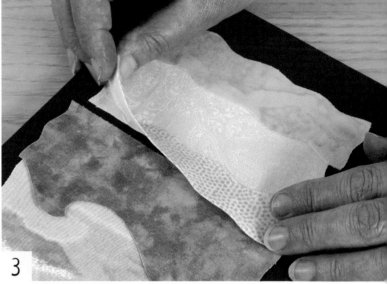

3

Position the background patches on the front of the notebook and glue them in place. Make sure that the waves on patch 2 overlap the sky (patch 1), and that patch 3 overlaps patches 2 and 4.

4

Trace or photocopy the bodice, collar and bloomer templates on page 46 and cut them out. Decide which patch of fabric you are using for which part of the design, and use the same technique as before to stiffen the fabrics and cut out the shapes.

Smart Stitch

If you want to use buttons or charms that have shanks on the design, remove the shanks with pliers to leave a flat surface so that you can stick them in place more easily.

5

Stick the shapes in position on the background to create the swimsuit shape, adding decorative cord or braid to the collar, perhaps with a little bow, and some scraps of lace to the bottoms of the bloomer legs.

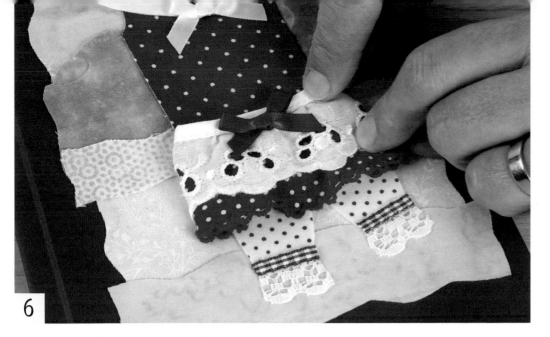

6

Embellish the frilled ribbon or braid if you wish, and stick it in place to create the skirt, folding the raw edges under at the sides and sticking them in position.

7

To finish, decorate the design with beads, buttons and charms or other embellishments of your choice.

Sailing By

Here's another design that conjures up lazy summer days. The background is created from the same templates as the main design, but this time all the shapes are cut from 'sky' and 'sea' fabrics. Use the boat templates on page 47 to cut patches from bright-coloured fabrics for the sails and wood-effect fabric for the hull, and stick them in place as before; note that patch 5 overlaps the bottom of the ship's hull. Instead of a strip of brown fabric you could use a toothpick as a mast. To finish, fill the sea with tiny fish to keep the boat company.

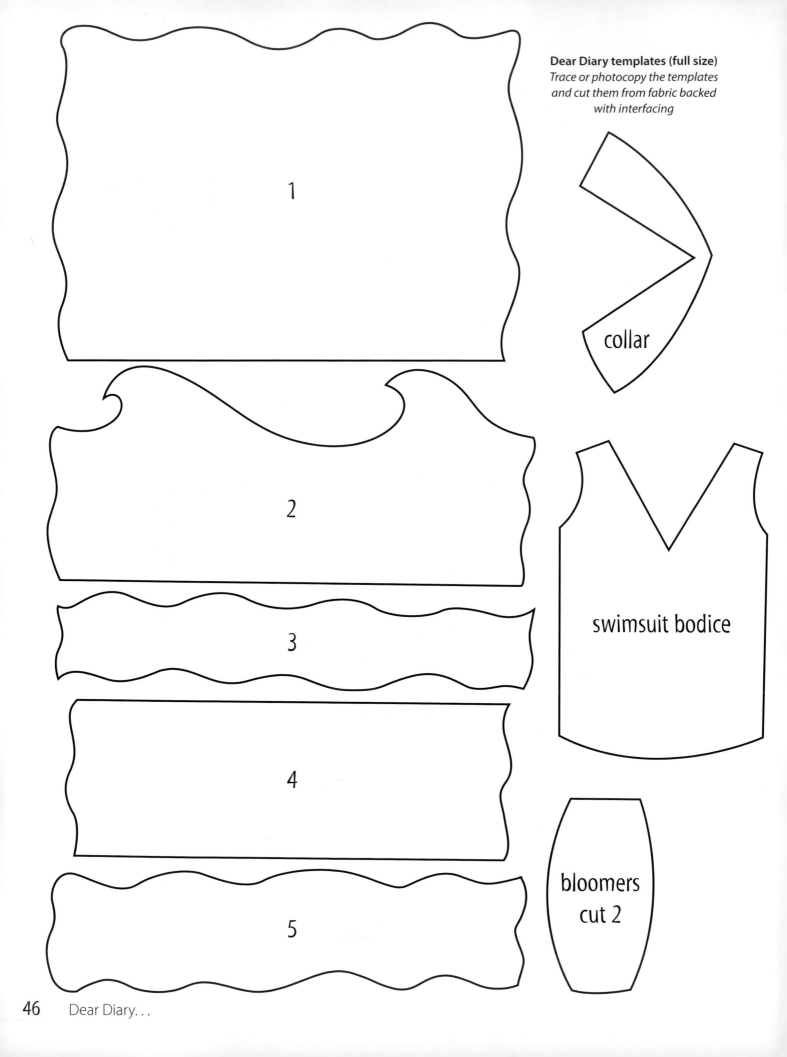

Dear Diary templates (full size)
*Trace or photocopy the templates
and cut them from fabric backed
with interfacing*

collar

1

2

3

4

5

swimsuit bodice

bloomers
cut 2

Sailing By templates (full size)
Use the background templates given for Dear Diary, cutting all the shapes from sea or sky fabrics, and stick them in place on the notebook. Trace or photocopy the other shapes and use them for the sails and hull of the boat

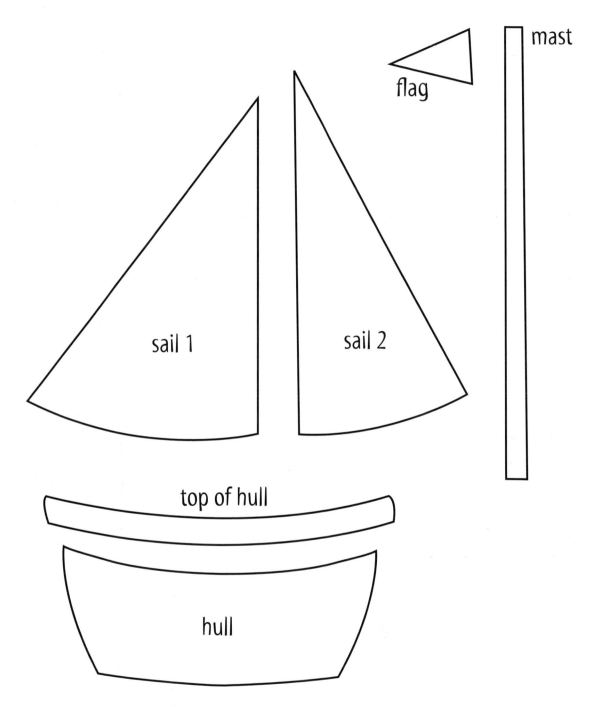

flag

mast

sail 1

sail 2

top of hull

hull

A Perfect Picture

A special photograph deserves a special frame, and this Jacobean-style appliqué design would make a wonderful wedding present. Why not work it in colours to match the outfits of the bride and groom? The design is built up in machine appliqué and embellished with toning beads. To ensure that the silk patches don't fray, I've fused them to the background with bonding web before doing the machine stitching. For a brighter folk-art version suitable for other occasions see page 51.

Easiness Rating ✶✶✶✶✶
Techniques Used Working with bonding web • Machine appliqué • Machine satin stitch
Finished Size Frame is 30 x 41cm (12 x 16in), to fit a photograph 20 x 25cm (8 x 10in)

You will need...

✓ Two 35 x 46cm (14 x 18in) rectangles of dark cream silk dupion

✓ Two 30 x 41cm (12 x 16in) rectangles of firm white cardboard

✓ 30 x 41cm (12 x 16in) compressed wadding (batting)

✓ 15 x 30cm (6 x 12in) Stitch 'n' Tear or white cartridge paper

✓ 15 x 30cm (6 x 12in) double-sided bonding web

✓ Scraps of silk dupion in assorted shades of your chosen colour scheme

✓ Sewing threads to complement silk fabrics and strong dark cream thread for joining frame

✓ Soft pencil and green pencil crayon

✓ Chalk marker

✓ Stick glue

✓ Sturdy craft knife

Press one of the silk rectangles and use a chalk marker to draw a rectangle 5cm (2in) in from the right-hand edge and the top and bottom edges. This rectangle marks the area that will be cut away to produce the frame; the blank area of fabric on the left will be decorated with the appliqué design. Trace or photocopy the main design on page 52. Lay the silk over the design so it is roughly 5cm (2in) from the top and bottom of the raw edge of the fabric and 4cm (1½in) in from the left-hand edge. Pin the layers together and use the green pencil crayon to trace all the lines of the design. ➤

2

Use a soft pencil to trace the templates from page 53 (the various parts of the main design) on to the paper side of the bonding web. Where a shape includes a second shape defined by a dotted line, trace the whole shape first, and then trace the area bordered by the dotted line separately to create a secondary template.

3

4

Cut the shapes out roughly and fuse them on to the backs of the chosen fabrics. Cut the patches out along the dotted lines. Peel away the backing papers and fuse these patches on to the traced design, fusing the secondary shapes on top of the main shapes.

Pin the piece of Stitch 'n' Tear (or cartridge paper) under the fused design and begin the appliqué. Set your sewing machine up for a small- to medium-width satin stitch and change the thread colours to suit the patches you are stitching. Stitch all the stems and tendrils first, tapering the tips of the tendrils as you near the end of the spiral (see page 117 for machine satin stitch). Appliqué all the different parts of the flowers and leaves. Once all stitching is finished, tear the foundation fabric or paper away from the design on the back of the work.

Smart Stitch

Cover your work surface with a soft towel while you're gluing the silk over the card; it's then easier to press the glued edges down firmly without squashing the beaded areas.

5

Embellish the design with beads; if you're not sure where the beads will work best, try different arrangements by laying them on the appliquéd design before you stitch.

6

To make up the frame, take one of the pieces of cardboard and draw a rectangle 5cm (2in) in from the right-hand edge and the top and bottom edges, just as you did on the piece of silk in step 1. Round the corners, then cut around the drawn line with a craft knife to create an aperture. Spread glue on the front of the cardboard shape and lay the wadding (batting) on top. Once the glue is dry, cut away the wadding inside the aperture.

7

Lay the appliqué design over the wadding so that the chalk lines coincide with the edges of the aperture; use a couple of pins to pin the fabric to the wadding so that the design doesn't move while you are gluing. Turn the whole project over; fold the raw edges of the silk to the back of the card shape and glue them in place. Once the glued edges are dry, use small, sharp-pointed scissors to cut away the silk to within 1.25cm (½in) of the edge of the aperture. Clip into the curved corners, clipping to just short of the edge of the card, then fold the raw edges of the silk over the edges of the aperture and glue them to the back of the cardboard.

8

Cover the remaining piece of cardboard with the remaining piece of silk, gluing the edges to the back of the card. Put the front and back of the frame together, right sides out, and use strong, dark cream thread to oversew the edges together, making sure that you leave the area above the aperture open. Once the pieces are joined, finish by slipping the photograph between the layers so that it appears in the aperture.

Folk-Art Fantasy

Favourite folk-art motifs of a bird, a heart and a flower are brought together in this alternative design for the photograph frame. The cheerful colour scheme of blue, pink and yellow would work well for a photograph of a new baby or a toddler – or you could try it in shades of purple and pink, or red and green. The frame is made in the same way as the main project, using the design and bonding web templates on pages 54 and 55.

A Perfect Picture template (full size)
Trace or photocopy the design and use a coloured pencil crayon to trace it on to the background silk

**A Perfect Picture
bonding web templates (full size)**
*Trace these shapes on to the paper side
of the bonding web; where a patch
includes a dotted shape, trace the solid
shape as one patch and the dotted
shape as a separate one*

**Folk-Art Fantasy template
(full size)**
*Trace or photocopy the design
and use a coloured pencil
crayon to trace it on to the
background silk*

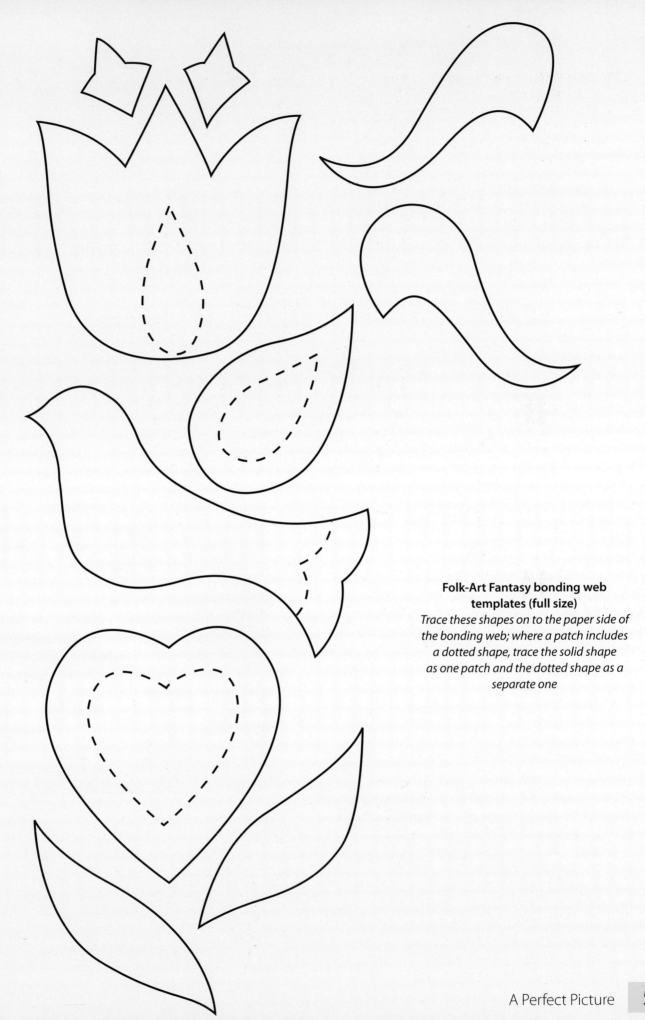

Folk-Art Fantasy bonding web templates (full size)
Trace these shapes on to the paper side of the bonding web; where a patch includes a dotted shape, trace the solid shape as one patch and the dotted shape as a separate one

Christmas Candy

Sweet treats abound at Christmas time so why not store them in a novelty bonbon box? This box, in a Christmas tree shape, can double as a table centrepiece and would look great on a buffet table. The box is made from fusible interfacing, which is soft enough to stitch but firm enough to create crisp shapes. Decorate your box with shiny baubles, candy-stick charms, snowflake buttons or even a string of miniature Christmas lights! I've also designed a fun rocket version on page 59 – perfect for children.

Easiness Rating ✳✳✳✳
Techniques Used Working with fusible interfacing • Making 3D shapes • Machine satin stitch
Finished Size 30cm (12in) tall and 15cm (6in) wide

You will need...

✓ 43 x 25cm (17 x 10in) green Christmas-print fabric for the tree

✓ Two 30 x 15cm (12 x 6in) rectangles and two 13cm (5in) squares of brown print cotton fabric

✓ Double-sided Fast2Fuse (see Suppliers) or other firm fusible interfacing:
  • 43 x 25cm (17 x 10in) rectangle
  • 30 x 15cm (12 x 6in) rectangle
  • 13cm (5in) square

✓ Green and brown sewing threads

✓ 80cm (32in) gold ribbon, 2.5cm (1in) wide

✓ Christmas charms, beads, sequins and miniature lights

✓ A3 sheet of paper, pencil, ruler, set of compasses

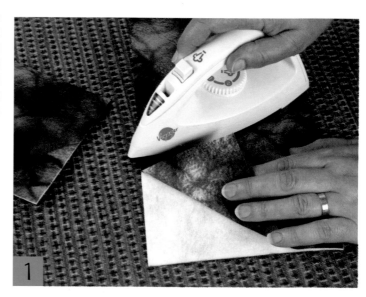

Lay one rectangle of brown fabric right side down on the ironing board and position the smaller rectangle of Fast2Fuse (or other firm double-sided fusible interfacing) on top, aligning the raw edges. Lay the other rectangle of brown fabric on top, right side up, and fuse the layers together with a warm iron. Do the same with the squares of brown fabric and the square of interfacing. ➤

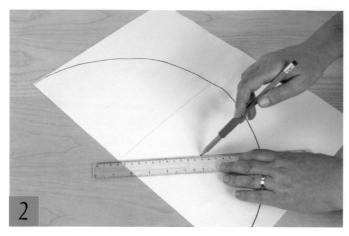

Draw a semicircle with a radius of 20cm (8in) on the paper. Divide it in half and then divide one of these halves roughly in half with a straight line (you don't need to be too exact as the angle isn't crucial). Cut out this shape.

Fuse the green fabric on to one side of the large piece of Fast2Fuse, and then use the paper template you made in step 2 as a guide to cut out the curved shape.

Smart Stitch

As the other side of the Fast2Fuse is also fusible, protect the ironing board with a non-stick ironing sheet as you fuse on the green fabric.

Using sharp scissors, cut a wavy line along the curved edge of the green shape. Make sure that the two straight edges of the shape measure the same after you have cut the wavy line; if not, even them up.

Set your sewing machine up to a medium-width zigzag and stitch round the edges of the stiffened green shape and the brown rectangle. If threads of fabric tend to peek out from the stitched edges, go round the shapes a second time to neaten them.

Follow the instructions in the panel opposite to create a tube from the brown shape, cutting and inserting the circular end as shown. Make a cone from the green shape.

7

Decorate the green cone with your chosen embellishments. To finish, tie the gold ribbon round the centre of the trunk and tie in a bow, trimming the ends at an angle.

Ready for Launch!

Any child will love this rocket filled with candies as the centrepiece for a birthday tea. I made the tube taller and thinner than the Christmas tree trunk, using a 19 x 25cm (7½ x 10in) rectangle of interfacing covered with silver fabric, and used bonding web to fuse on a line of 'flames' cut from red metallic fabric. As metallic fabrics are not as easy to stitch as cottons, I sealed the back of the tube and neatened the top and bottom edges with ribbon. For the top I used the same curved shape that I drew for the Christmas tree, but without trimming the edge into a wavy line.

In a nutshell…

Creating 3D shapes

Fast2Fuse is a wonderful material for shaping into bowls and boxes. Follow these instructions to make a tube and a cone – both shapes can be altered in size and proportion but the construction principle remains the same. If you gently bend each covered piece of interfacing before you stitch it, it will help to produce a smoothly curved shape rather than stiff folds.

1 To make a cylinder, lace the two short edges of a covered rectangle to each other with ladder stitch (see page 117). Take a horizontal stitch into each edge alternately and after a few stitches pull the thread tight to bring the edges together.

2 Once the rectangle has been stitched into a tube, make sure that the shape is nice and circular then stand it on the covered square of interfacing. Draw around the end of the tube and use this line as a guide to cut the end circle.

3 Go round the edge of the circle with satin stitch and then insert it in one end of the tube and use ladder stitch to join the two edges.

4 To make the cone shape, bring the two straight edges together and secure them firmly at the bottom, then lace the straight edges together with ladder stitch.

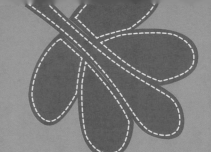

Go for Glitz

Simple strip patchwork is transformed into something special by the use of ribbons and braids in this glitzy evening bag. Hand embroidery and quick Prairie Points add texture, while beads and fake jewels provide finishing touches. Use silk dupion for the Prairie Points; it has a wonderful sheen and is easy to press into sharp points. The bag has a zip at the back, so all your bits and pieces are kept safe while you party! Make the bag in colours to match a special evening dress – and stitch a little change purse to match.

Easiness Rating ✷✷✷✷
Techniques Used Simple strip patchwork • Quick Prairie Points • Hand embroidery • Inserting a zip
Finished Size 20 x 15cm (8 x 6in)

You will need...
for the bag

- ✓ 30 x 23cm (12 x 9in) firm foundation fabric
- ✓ 30 x 23cm (12 x 9in) lining fabric
- ✓ 23cm (9in) strips of assorted ribbons and braids in toning colours
- ✓ 23cm (9in) strips of quick Prairie Points in silk dupion (follow panel on page 63)
- ✓ 20cm (8in) zip fastener in a toning colour
- ✓ Stranded embroidery threads or coton perlé in toning colours
- ✓ Assorted toning beads, sequins and fake jewels
- ✓ Sewing threads to suit your colour scheme
- ✓ Fine invisible thread (optional)

1

To make the bag, lay the piece of foundation fabric on a flat surface and pin on the strips of ribbon in a pleasing order, overlapping the edges slightly. At the top and bottom of the rectangle, use wide ribbons and ensure that they extend beyond the raw edge of the foundation fabric by about 1.25cm (½in). Once you're happy with the arrangement, trap the raw edges of the Prairie Point strips you made between some of the ribbons and pin lengths of braid over others. Position the Prairie Points so they face downwards on the front and back of the bag. ➤

Glitzy Bitz

The little purse (shown right) is made in the same way as the bag but smaller. Work on a 16 x 18cm (6½ x 7in) rectangle of foundation fabric, using 16cm (6½in) strips of ribbon, braid and Prairie Points, and insert a 10cm or 12.5cm (4in or 5in) zip.

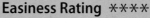

Machine stitch the ribbons where they overlap, so that you're appliquéing them to the foundation fabric and trapping the Prairie Points. You can either use a toning colour for each ribbon, or thread the machine with invisible thread and use that for all the ribbons. Once all the ribbons are secured, stitch on the braids. Add lines of hand embroidery to some of the ribbons – I used feather stitch, whipped running stitch, curved lines of fern stitch and star shapes made of straight stitches (see Useful Stitches pages 116 and 119).

Lay the appliqué design right side down and cover it with the lining fabric, right side up, with raw edges aligning (the edges of the top and bottom ribbon strips will extend beyond the fabric). Fold these edges over to the front of the lining fabric and slipstitch in place to create bound edges.

Fold the design into a tube, right side out, and stitch the zip fastener between the bound edges, positioning it so that the ends of the zip are even distances from the raw edges of the design. You can use either hand stitching or machine stitching to secure the zip.

Smart Stitch

If you are sewing the zip fastener into your bag by machine, use the zipper foot to make the task easier.

Open the zip part-way, and turn the tube wrong side out. Fold it flat, so that the zip is slightly below the top fold as shown, and stitch the side seams by machine, taking a 1.25cm (½in) seam. Make sure that you've opened the zip before you do these seams, otherwise you won't be able to turn the bag to the right side!

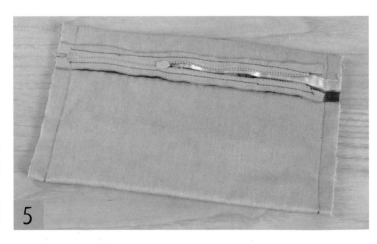

6

Clip the corners and turn the bag right way out. Using a cool iron, press just the very edges of the bag to set the folds. If you think that any of the ribbons won't take the heat of the iron, finger-press the folds firmly instead, as shown in the circular detail.

7

Finish your bag by embellishing it with beads, sequins, fake jewels and so on.

In a nutshell... Quick Prairie Points

If you'd like a strip of Prairie Points, as opposed to individual ones (see page 14), try this method; it produces a line of crisp points at even intervals and is much faster than making the points singly. Here I've given instructions for the size of points I used for the bag but you can make the points smaller or larger – just ensure that the depth of the cuts is half the distance between the points.

1 Cut a fabric strip 5cm (2in) wide and press under one long edge.

2 At 5cm (2in) intervals, cut down into the folded edge to a depth of 2.5cm (1in).

3 Fold the edges of each cut section diagonally to the centre to create a point and then press firmly.

4 Once you have pressed all the points, stitch a line of machine zigzag along the folded raw edges to secure them. When you use the strips, ensure that that the raw edges and the machine stitching are hidden between the layers of ribbon.

Little Treasures

The years of babyhood are over so quickly, but before they disappear make sure you have a special place to keep baby's memorabilia – the hospital wrist-band and footprint, the first pair of bootees, the cards that come with the congratulations bouquets, a lock of baby hair. . . Tuck them safely into a decorated box. Then, when your teenager brings home that first boyfriend or girlfriend, you can bring out your treasures box to embarrass them! There's a jazzier version of the box on page 67.

Easiness Rating ✱✱
Techniques Used Simple machine patchwork
Finished Size 20cm (8in) square; for a smalller or larger lid, reduce or enlarge templates

You will need...

✓ Scraps of cotton fabrics in assorted mid-pastel plains and prints (I used 12 different ones but you could use fewer)

✓ Four 21.5 x 5.5cm (8½ x 2¼in) strips of plain fabric

✓ 20cm (8in) square of thick card

✓ 20cm (8in) square of 2oz wadding (batting)

✓ Assorted baby charms and buttons in pastel colours

✓ White sewing thread and coloured threads to match charms and buttons

✓ Stick glue and strong clear glue

✓ 1m (1yd) white cord

✓ Scrap of brown paper or thin card for a label

1

Cut a snippet of each patchwork fabric and use the small grid on page 67 to try out arrangements for the patchwork. Once you're happy with the arrangement, stick a snippet in the appropriate square or triangle; this will remind you of the order in which to join the patches. I used the arrangement shown here and pieced each half of the final square in the same pattern. ➤

Trace or photocopy the templates, opposite, and cut them out. Use the templates to cut patches from the appropriate fabrics; these templates include seam allowances, so you don't need to add any extra fabric around the edges. Begin at one end of row A, and begin joining the patches in the order you have chosen; stitch with 6mm (¼in) seams and press each seam open as you stitch. Make two A strips in this way.

Join the patches of row B in the same way, and then make another copy of row B.

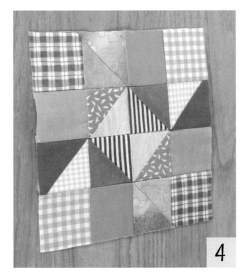

Now join the rows in the correct order to complete the patchwork square.

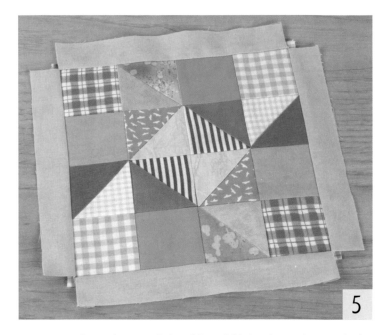

On each strip of plain fabric, fold the short edges under by 6mm (¼in) to give you a 20cm (8in) strip, and press. Seam these strips to the edges of the patchwork square.

Smart Stitch

Keep checking your small layout, to ensure that you join the rows in the correct order; it's easy to join the wrong edges of the pieced strips together if you don't concentrate!

Spread some stick glue on to the card square and press the wadding (batting) firmly on top. Once the glue is dry, lay the patchwork square right side down and lay the card square on top, wadding side down. Fold the raw edges of the fabric strips over the card and glue them in place, checking that the edges of the patchwork square align with the edges of the card.

7

Spread a generous layer of strong, clear glue on the back of the card and when the glue is nearly dry, press the square in place on the box top.

8

Decorate the lid with charms and buttons, and then neaten the glued edge with white cord. Tie the cord at one corner and add a label with the baby's name or a little photograph.

Little Treasures templates (full size)
Trace or photocopy the templates and then cut them out; use them as guides for cutting the squares and triangles from the patchwork fabrics

Patchwork grid
Use this small grid to try out arrangements for the patchwork – see step 1

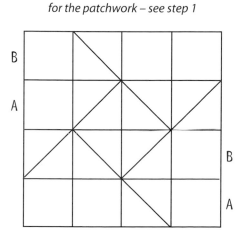

All the Colours of the Rainbow

Use jazzy cottons and a brightly coloured box to create a treasures box for an older child. I've pieced this version of the design from a rainbow of bright fabrics, working across the spectrum from one corner of the block to the other. The finished design is decorated with a mixture of quirky charms and buttons, and the lid edged with a woven ribbon twisted into a cord.

Heart to Heart

Celtic knots have a timeless appeal and this modern version has all the beauty of the ancient designs created by Celtic artists. A circle of woven hearts is a perfect symbol for a marriage and seems just right to grace a bridal bag. The design is worked in corded (Italian) quilting and the channels for the cord are stitched in variegated thread in a pretty mix of pinks, blues and lilacs. The finished pattern is set off by opalescent beads and beaded heart charms. Check out the gorgeous scarlet version on page 73.

Easiness Rating ✳✳✳✳
Techniques Used Hand embroidery • Corded (Italian) quilting
Finished Size The bag front is roughly 18 x 20cm (7 x 8in)

You will need...

- ✓ Four 25cm (10in) squares of ivory silk dupion
- ✓ 25cm (10in) square of firm white cotton fabric
- ✓ Four 20cm (8in) squares of double-sided Fast2Fuse (see Suppliers) or other firm fusible interfacing
- ✓ Variegated fine coton perlé
- ✓ Small amount of knitting wool in a pale colour
- ✓ Opalescent beads and six heart charms
- ✓ 60cm (24in) ivory cotton lace
- ✓ 50cm (20in) fine white cord
- ✓ Large-eyed embroidery needle and a large tapestry needle
- ✓ Sewing threads to match beads and charms
- ✓ Strong white sewing thread and tacking thread
- ✓ Pale blue pencil crayon

1

Trace or photocopy the whole design on page 71. Lay one of the squares of dupion over the design and use the blue pencil crayon to trace just the knot design (not the dotted hexagon shape). ➤

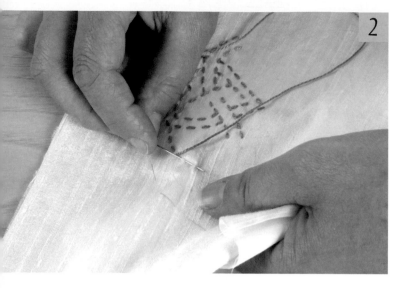

2

Position the firm white fabric behind the marked fabric square and tack (baste) the two layers together around the edge of the design. Using one strand of the coton perlé and the large-eyed embroidery needle, stitch around all of the lines of the design with a medium-length running stitch (see page 118). The large-eyed needle ensures that you can pull the relatively thick thread through the fine fabric smoothly.

Once the design is stitched, lay it face down on a soft towel and press it gently from the back with a cool iron. Follow the corded quilting instructions in the panel on page 72 to thread the channels with wool to produce the raised knot design.

3

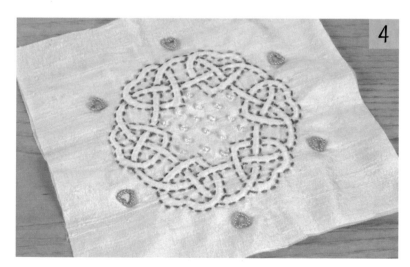

4

Embellish the knot design with beads and charms. I filled the central shape with a scattering of opalescent beads and then stitched six beaded hearts around the perimeter of the design.

Cut the hexagon shape out of the paper template and use this to cut four hexagon shapes from the squares of Fast2Fuse. Lay the stitched design face down on a flat surface and position one of the fusible hexagons centrally over it. Trim the edges of the fabrics to about 1.25cm (½in) outside the hexagon. Fold the raw edges of the backing fabric firmly over to the back of the hexagon and fuse into place with a warm iron, folding the corners crisply. Once you've fused all the edges of the backing fabric, use stick glue to fix the raw edges of the silk to the back of the hexagon. Use the remaining squares of silk dupion to cover the other hexagons, trimming the fabric to 1.25cm (½in) outside the hexagon and then fusing the raw edges to the back. Give each of these covered shapes a quick press with a cool iron on the right side to fuse the silk firmly to the front and create a flat finish.

5

Work the running stitches relatively loosely, then the fabric won't distort when you thread the stitched channels.

Heart to Heart template (full size)
Trace or photocopy the design and trace the knot only on to the silk dupion. Cut round the dotted hexagon and use this shape as a template for cutting the fusible interfacing

Corded quilting

This technique produces raised channels on the front of the work. The channels are padded by threading them from the back with wool or fine cord. Use a firm fabric for the backing fabric so it provides a flat background to throw the corded design into relief.

1 Patterns suitable for corded quilting are made up of a series of stitched channels, worked on two layers of fabric together. Many Celtic knots lend themselves well to this kind of quilting.

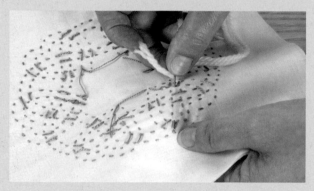

2 Thread a tapestry needle with two strands of knitting wool. Working on the back of the design, thread each stitched channel by taking the tapestry needle into just the backing fabric, making sure that the needle doesn't come through the front fabric.

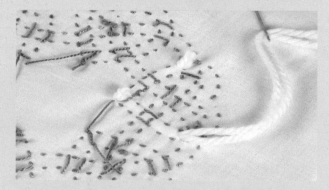

3 When you reach a corner, such as the point of each heart, bring the needle out through the cotton fabric and re-insert it, leaving a small loop of wool so the point is well padded. Once all the channels have been threaded, the padding will produce a raised design on the right side of the work.

6

Put the embroidered hexagon together with one of the other covered hexagons, wrong sides together, and oversew around the edges, leaving 1.25cm (½in) unstitched at each end of the top edge, to slip in the ends of the cord later on. Oversew the remaining two covered hexagons together, without leaving any gaps. Put the two sides of the bag together, right sides out, and pin the lace between the layers around every side except the top. Stitch the layers together around those sides, securing the lace as you go. Trim the cord to the length you want and insert the raw ends into the gaps at the bag top. Stitch the gaps closed, catching the cord securely as you stitch.

Silk Sizzler

You don't have to stitch this design in pastel colours; it looks glorious in a sizzling mixture of red silk and multicoloured thread. If you find it difficult to see the design through the darker silk, pin the fabric and the paper design together and then tape them to a window on a bright day – or use a light-box if you have one. For this version I've used a single length of multicoloured braid for the bag handle and to decorate the edges, and embellished the central design with glimmering beads in rich colours. Little clusters of beads around the edge of the knot provide the perfect finishing touch.

No Place Like Home

In this delightful folksy picture, a quirky little house nestles in its own garden surrounded by a white picket fence. I've made it in country-style prints and plaids, embellished with buttons and charms. The fabric patches are cut deliberately uneven to increase the whimsical look of the finished picture, and then appliquéd to the background with large running stitches in coton à broder. For a really quick project, stitch just the house – see page 78.

Easiness Rating ✳✳✳
Techniques Used Using double-sided bonding web • Folk-art appliqué
Finished Size 35 x 28cm (14 x 11in)

You will need...

✓ Iron-on interfacing ½m (½yd)

✓ Cotton fabrics as follows (use a mixture of plains, small prints and plaids):
  • 33 x 26cm (13 x 10in) pale blue background fabric (also acts as sky)
  • 23 x 16cm (9 x 6in) pale green for hills
  • 23 x 13cm (9 x 5in) medium green for grass
  • 16 x 13cm (6 x 5in) tan check for house
  • 16 x 10cm (6 x 4in) red print for roof
  • 12 x 4cm (4½ x 1½in) yellow print for windows
  • 5cm (2in) square of mottled blue for door
  • 12 x 8cm (4½ x 3in) green print for tree
  • 9cm (3½in) square of mottled brown for path
  • 23 x 10cm (9 x 4in) white for cloud and fence
  • 6.5cm (2½in) square of yellow for sun
  • 10cm (4in) square of pale orange for sun's rays
  • 4cm (1½in) square of dark orange for sun details
  • 10 x 5cm (4 x 2in) brown print for roof struts, chimney and tree trunk
  • 15cm (6in) of cream lace for window-blinds
  • Two different tan or wood-effect fabrics, one 36 x 18cm (14 x 7in) rectangle of each for 'frames'

✓ Rotary cutter, cutting mat and quilters' rule

✓ Coton à broder in assorted colours to tone (or contrast) with the fabric patches

✓ Assorted garden-style charms and buttons, plus matching threads

✓ Wooden picture frame with an aperture roughly 35 x 28cm (14 x 11in)

✓ Glue or strong tape for mounting

1

Cut a piece of interfacing to fit each of the fabric pieces except the blue background and the lace for the blinds. Use a warm iron to fuse each piece of interfacing on to the wrong side of the appropriate fabric. ➤

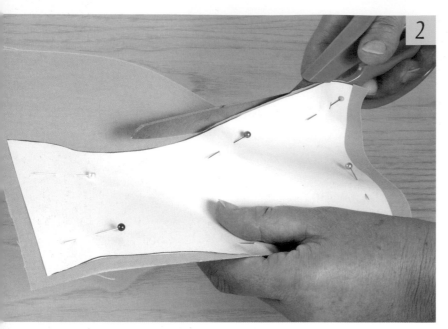

2

Trace or photocopy the template on page 79 twice. On one copy, cut along the dotted lines across the design (marked green on the master diagram) to create the hill and grass shapes: discard the rest of this copy. Use these two shapes as templates to cut patches from the hill and grass fabrics. Pin each template right side up on the right side of the fabric and cut around the edge. When you're cutting the straight edge of the hills, add an extra 6mm (¼in) of fabric so this piece will tuck beneath the grass shape.

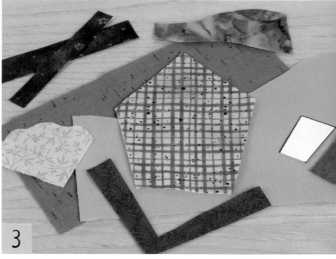

3

Cut up the second copy of the design to create templates for the house, roof, path, chimney, cloud, tree, tree trunk and the background shapes for the sun and its rays. Don't cut out the windows of the house or the decorative patches on the sun yet. (Note: you don't need to cut templates for the fence – see step 4.) Use all these templates to cut patches from the appropriate fabrics; add about 6mm (¼in) to the top edges of the house shape, so that it will tuck securely under the roof patch.

4

Trim the remaining white fabric into a rectangle and then use a rotary cutter to cut it into uneven strips to use later for the picket fence.

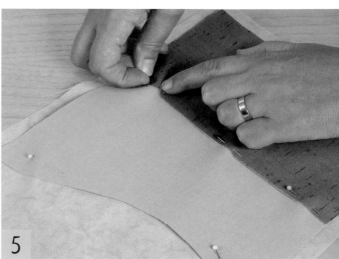

5

Pin the grass and hill shapes on to the blue background fabric, overlapping the fabric patches slightly where they join.

Cut the strips of white fabric to different lengths, cutting the ends at angles so they are uneven in size and shape, and then pin them on to the background for the rails and posts of the fence. Pin on the house, the path and the cloud, and then the background pieces of the sun and its rays.

From the paper house shape, cut out the windows, door and roof struts and use these shapes to cut patches from the appropriate fabrics. Do the same with the decorative patches on the sun and its rays. Pin each one in place on the design.

Smart Stitch

If you want to quilt the entire design, add compressed wadding or curtain interlining behind the blue fabric before working the running stitches.

Using coton à broder, work a medium-sized running stitch round the edges of each shape to appliqué it into place. You could match the colours of the thread to each patch or use a contrasting colour. Remove all pins when this stitching is finished.

Use the rotary cutter, board and ruler to trim the edges of the blue fabric so they are roughly similar to the angles on the design, to create a quirky shape for the central panel. Cut each rectangle of wood-effect 'frame' fabric roughly in half, cutting at a slight angle down the length. Add the strips of frame fabric to the sides of the design first, and then to the top and bottom, appliquéing them in position with running stitch.

Cut three short lengths of lace and stitch one to the top of each window shape.

Using matching threads, stitch the charms and buttons on to the grass and tree. Frame the picture by laying the design right side down on a flat surface; position the backboard of the frame on top so there's an even border of fabric all round. Fold the raw edges of the design over the edges of the board and stick neatly in place with glue or strong tape. The picture looks more attractive without glass.

Welcome to Your New Home

For this variation of the main project I've omitted the background details and stitched the house on its own, appliquéd to some floral print fabric. Stitch in the same way as the main project and use the same template. This design would make a lovely little card or picture – ideal as a moving house present. You could also use it as a patch on a ready-made bag.

Smart Stitch

To give my picture a slightly padded appearance, I stuck a rectangle of 2oz wadding (batting) on the front of the frame's backboard before stretching the design over it.

No Place Like Home template (full size)
Make two copies of the template, and cut one along the green lines marked (solid and dotted) to produce large shapes for the hill and grass. Cut up the other copy to produce templates for the sun, cloud, house, tree and path; you don't need individual templates for the fence

Daisy, Daisy...

Sumptuous cream and gold fabric creates a rich surface for this trinket bowl, made in the shape of a daisy and stiffened with interfacing. The petals are stitched individually and neatened with machine satin stitch before being stitched to the central circle. Once the petals are in place it's a simple matter to join them to create the bowl shape. You'll soon be ready to stitch a whole bouquet of flowers – see the dramatic anemone bowls on page 85.

Easiness Rating ✳✳✳
Techniques Used Using double-sided bonding web • Machine satin stitch
Finished Size 20cm (8in) diameter

You will need...

✓ Two 51 x 6.5cm (20 x 2½in) strips of cream/gold fabric for petals

✓ Two 10cm (4in) squares of pale yellow fabric for flower centre

✓ Two 51 x 6.5cm (20 x 2½in) strips and two 10cm (4in) squares of double-sided bonding web

✓ One 51 x 6.5cm (20 x 2½in) strip and one 10cm (4in) square of Timtex, pelmet Vilene, or similar heavyweight interfacing

✓ Large spool of bright yellow machine sewing thread

✓ Orange/yellow pencil

✓ Pearls or other beads for embellishment

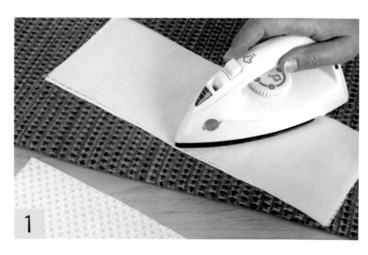

1

Lay one strip of cream/gold fabric right side down on an ironing board and lay a strip of bonding web, glue (rough) side down on top so that the edges align. Fuse the web in place with a warm iron. Fuse the remaining strip of web on to the back of the other strip of petal fabric in the same way. ➤

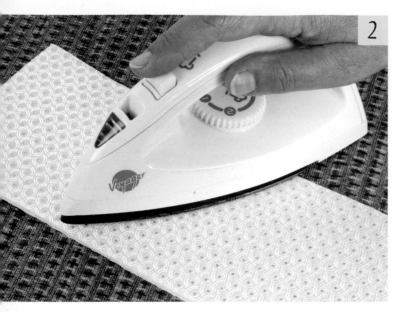

2

Peel the backing paper away from one of the bonded pieces and lay the fabric right side up on the Timtex strip. Fuse the fabric into place with a warm iron. Add the second piece of fabric to the other side of the Timtex strip in the same way.

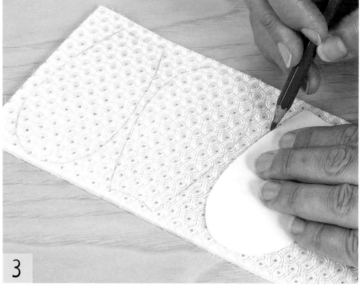

3

Trace or photocopy the daisy templates A and B below and, using the coloured pencil, draw round petal template A nine times on to the covered Timtex shape.

4

Use sharp fabric scissors to cut out all the petal shapes.

B

Daisy Daisy templates (full size)
Use for the petals and flower centre

A

5

Cover both sides of the Timtex square with yellow fabric in same way. Trace template B, the central circle, on to one side and cut out the shape.

6

Set your sewing machine to a medium-width satin stitch (about 3.5) or a close zigzag. Edge each petal with bright yellow satin stitch (see page 117), working so that the outer edge of the satin stitch goes just over the edge of the petal shape. Don't stitch the bottom edges of the petals.

7

Pin the petals evenly around the central circle, trimming the circle very slightly if necessary to make the petals fit

8 Set your machine to a medium zigzag (about 3 width and length) and stitch round the edge of the circle once or twice to attach the petals. Re-set the machine for satin stitch or close zigzag (width about 4), and stitch round the edge of the circle.

Daisy, Daisy. . .   83

9 Pull each pair of petals together gently and stitch up from the centre with a small zigzag to create the bowl shape; joining the petals for about 2.5cm (1in) will produce nicely curved sides.

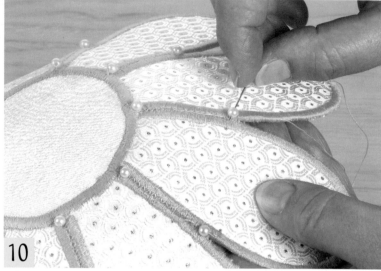

10

Sew on pearl beads to decorate the bowl – I added a bead to the top and bottom of each seam between the petals, on both the inside and the outside of the bowl.

Smart Stitch

The longer you make the line of zigzag between the petals, the steeper the sides of your bowl will be.

Stained-Glass Anemones

These dramatic anemone bowls are made in the same way as the daisy bowl but use templates C and D, given here. For each bowl make five petals in pink or purple batik fabric, and use black thread to stitch the petals around a mottled black central circle. You can then decorate the inside of each petal with 'stamens' formed from lines of backstitch topped with black seed beads.

C

D

Stained Glass Anemones templates (full size)
Use for petals and flower centre

Lavender's Blue

These gorgeous little sachets made from pretty batik fabric let the scent of lavender or pot-pourri float out from the organza mesh in the centre. This unusual central feature also provides an opportunity for some lovely decorative embroidery and embellishment. A beautiful cinnamon-coloured version on page 90 uses chunky wood shavings for a spicier aroma but you could also use herbs.

Easiness Rating ✳✳
Techniques Used Simple reverse appliqué • Hand embroidery • Tassel making
Finished Size 18cm (7in) square

You will need...

for one bag

- ✓ Two 23cm (9in) squares of purple batik fabric
- ✓ 15cm (6in) square of toning sheer gauze or organza
- ✓ 50cm (20in) narrow cream braid
- ✓ Cream stranded embroidery cotton (floss) or coton perlé
- ✓ Sewing threads to tone with fabric and braid
- ✓ Small cream ribbon bow
- ✓ Toning beads for decorating the central panel
- ✓ Lavender (or pot-pourri) and small amount of polyester stuffing
- ✓ Four large pearl beads and four tassels (ready-bought or homemade)
- ✓ Soft pencil and soft pale crayon

1

Trace or photocopy the curved shape on page 91 and cut it out, including the centre part. ➤

2

Lay one of the batik squares right side down, centre the template on top and trace round the inside and outside of the shape in soft pencil.

Pin the patch of sheer fabric over the inner line of the design and, using pale thread (so that you can see the stitches easily), work a line of small zigzag stitches around the inner pencil line.

3

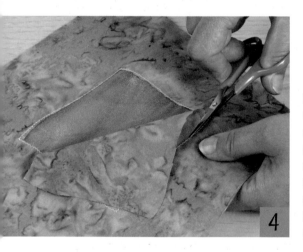

4

On the right side of the work, separate the layers of fabric inside the line of zigzag and carefully cut away just the batik fabric. Cut as close to the zigzag as you comfortably can, but make sure that you don't cut the sheer fabric.

5

Use a pale crayon to mark wavy lines across the central shape at the halfway and quarter points in each direction to create a grid of curved lines.

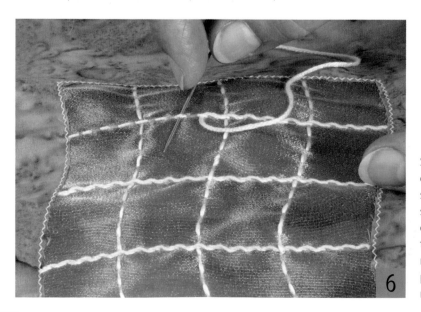

6

Still on the right side of the work, use six strands of cream stranded cotton or coton à broder to work whipped running stitch (see page 118) along these marked lines.

7 On the right side of the work, use a small zigzag stitch to appliqué cream braid round the edge of the central shape, starting and finishing at a corner and stitching over the braid several times where the ends join. Trim off the braid ends and neaten the join by sewing on a small bow. Decorate the design on the sheer fabric with beads: I created simple flower motifs using a coloured pearl and four petal-shaped beads for each flower.

Smart Stitch

If the lavender or pot-pourri doesn't look very attractive through the sheer fabric, make sure that the stuffing is at the top so that it shows through the mesh instead.

8 Make up the sachet by pinning the batik squares right sides together and stitching round the outer wavy line, leaving about 10cm (4in) open for turning. Trim the edges to 6mm (¼in) beyond the pencil line and clip the corners and curves.

9 Turn the shape to the right side, pushing the corners out to neat points. Fill the bag softly with a mixture of lavender (or pot-pourri) and polyester stuffing and then slipstitch the opening closed.

10

To finish off, add a bead and tassel at each corner – see panel, right, for making tassels.

Cinnamon Sachet

For this variation of the sachet I've used a colour scheme of gold and burnt orange, stuffed with scented wood shavings. The decoration in the sheer window is simply lengths of twisted cord sewn into place with a jewel in the centre. You could also make your own cord – see page 101. Instead of thread tassels at the corners I've sewn on small beaded tassels, easily made from a selection of mixed beads.

Making tassels

Tassels are a simple but effective finishing touch for many projects. This technique allows you to make two at a time.

1 Decide how long you'd like your tassels to be and cut a piece of firm card to a width slightly over twice this measurement. Choose assorted threads (different types, thicknesses and colours) that tone with your fabrics and wrap them round the card several times – the more times you wrap them, the thicker your final tassels will be.

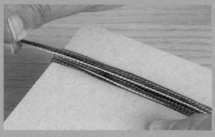

2 Thread a tapestry needle with toning thread, feed it through the loops at one edge of the card and tie tightly. Do the same at the other edge.

3 Cut the loops of thread halfway between the ties on one side of the card and then on the other side at the same level. Remove the card.

4 Smooth one tassel down, then use the needle and thread to stitch into the tassel head and wind a thread tightly around the cords near the top. Secure the thread by taking it into the body of the tassel.

5 Finish the second tassel in the same way, then trim both tassels to the same length. Use the original tie as a thread for securing the tassel to your project, or if you prefer, cut it away and add beads or finer threads.

Lavender's Blue template (full size)
*Trace or photocopy the shape and use it as a
template for marking the batik fabric*

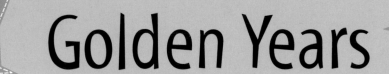

Golden Years

Commemorate a Golden Wedding anniversary with a beautiful decorated scrapbook, perfect for photographs, mementoes or anniversary cards. The Indian-style motif is created in simple stained-glass patchwork using fusible bias binding, and then embellished with gold and pearl beads. I've also stitched a paisley motif in greens, which would be suitable for an Emerald anniversary (see page 95), but of course you can vary the colours of either design to suit Silver, Pearl, Ruby, Emerald, Sapphire or Diamond celebrations.

Easiness Rating ✳✳
Techniques Used Simple machine appliqué • Simple stained-glass patchwork
Finished Size The padded motif is 24 x 16cm (9½ x 6¼in)

You will need...

✓ 30 x 22cm (12 x 8½in) embroidered cream silk dupion

✓ 13 x 8cm (5 x 3in) gold brocade fabric

✓ 30 x 22cm (12 x 8½in) compressed wadding (batting)

✓ 1.5m (1¾yd) gold fusible bias binding, 6mm (¼in) wide

✓ Golden-yellow sewing thread

✓ 30 x 22cm (12 x 8½in) piece of cardboard

✓ Stick glue and clear glue

✓ Toning beads, charms, sequins, fake jewels and matching sewing threads

✓ Golden or cream scrapbook or photo album, with a front cover at least 30 x 20cm (12 x 8in)

Trace or photocopy the motif on page 96. Lay the embroidered silk over the design, right side up, so that there is an even border of fabric all the way round the motif. Use a soft pencil to trace the solid lines of the design on to the silk. ➤

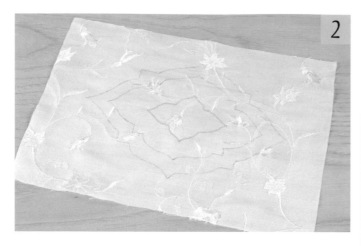

2

Position the gold fabric behind the centre of the motif, right side up, and pin it in place. Work a small machine zigzag stitch around the edge of the central shape.

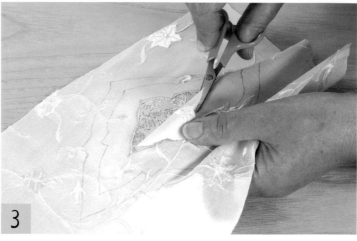

3

Using small, sharp-pointed embroidery scissors, carefully cut through just the cream fabric in the centre of the design. Cut away the cream silk just inside the line of zigzag. On the back of the work, trim away the excess gold fabric just outside the line of zigzag.

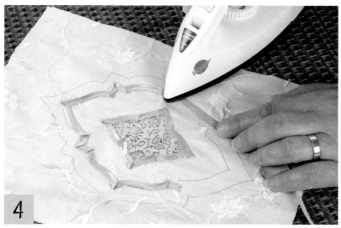

4

5

Working from the central line outwards, fuse gold bias binding over each marked line. Begin each line of binding at one of the right angles. When you've covered the drawn line and reached the starting point again, trim the binding 6mm (¼in) beyond the end of the line, then fold the end under and press it in place to neaten both raw ends.

Stitch the lines of binding in position. If you're stitching by hand, use a small slipstitch; if you're stitching by machine, use a tiny zigzag in a matching thread, or use invisible thread and a blind hemming stitch.

6

Embellish the design by sewing on beads, charms, sequins, fake jewels and so on.

Smart Stitch

At each corner, mitre the binding neatly to create a crisp fold. Fold it back on itself first of all, then fold it at 45° along the new edge.

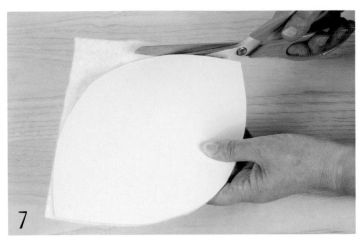

7

8

Cut your original paper design round the dotted line to give you the shape for the cardboard mount. Trace round this shape on to the cardboard and cut out. Spread one side of the card shape with a thin layer of stick glue and press the wadding on to it, trimming the wadding to fit the shape.

Stretch the embellished design over the wadding and glue the edges to the back of the card shape.

9

Use strong glue to stick the covered shape to the front of the scrapbook. Spread the back of the card with a generous layer of glue and leave it until almost dry before pressing it firmly to the front of the book; this way, you are much less likely to get excess glue squeezing out around the edge of the shape.

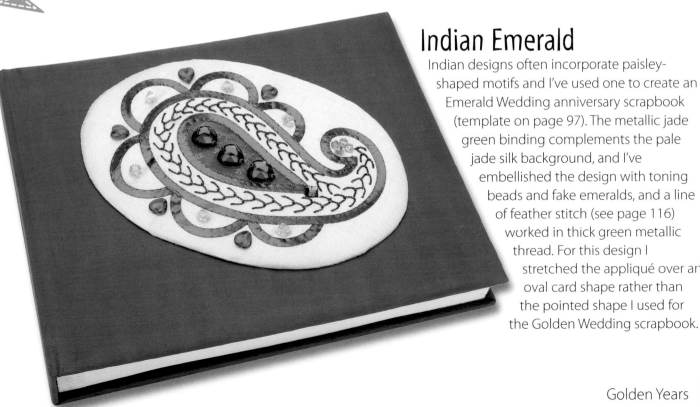

Indian Emerald

Indian designs often incorporate paisley-shaped motifs and I've used one to create an Emerald Wedding anniversary scrapbook (template on page 97). The metallic jade green binding complements the pale jade silk background, and I've embellished the design with toning beads and fake emeralds, and a line of feather stitch (see page 116) worked in thick green metallic thread. For this design I stretched the appliqué over an oval card shape rather than the pointed shape I used for the Golden Wedding scrapbook.

Golden Years template (full size)
Trace or photocopy the design. Trace the solid lines only on to the silk in pencil; use the dotted line as a template for cutting the card shape

Indian Emerald template (full size)
*Trace or photocopy the design.
Trace the solid lines only on to
the silk in pencil; use the dotted line as
a template for cutting the card shape*

Denim Delight

Little girls (and big ones too!) will love this denim shoulder bag, with its bright flower motif, buttons and matching cord strap. The decorative flower is created using the chenille technique, which involves stitching layers of fabric together and then slashing them on the bias so that the edges fray. The bag is simplicity itself to sew together – and do check out the zinging citrus alternative on page 101.

Easiness Rating ✳✳✳
Techniques Used Creating chenille • Big-stitch quilting • Twisted cord
Finished Size 18cm (7in) square approximately, excluding strap

You will need...

✓ Four 20cm (8in) squares of denim

✓ Three 16.5cm (6½in) squares of coloured cotton fabric: one pink, one mauve and one yellow/orange

✓ Soft white or yellow pencil

✓ Quilters' rule, with 6mm (¼in) increments

✓ Skein of variegated coton perlé in shades to tone with coloured fabrics

✓ Blue sewing thread and pale tacking (basting) thread

✓ Toning embellishments, such as buttons, charms and beads

✓ 130cm (50in) cord approx, either bought or home-made, for trim and shoulder strap

Trace or photocopy the template on page 102. Cut it out and then cut away the petals and flower centre to create a stencil. Place one square of denim right side up on a flat surface and position the stencil on top, so there's a roughly even border of fabric all the way around, and then trace round the shape with a pale pencil. Lay a quilters' rule across one diagonal of the square and draw a line within the shapes of the design. Work outwards in 6mm (¼in) increments to create a pattern of parallel lines across the petals and flower centre. ➤

2 Layer the coloured fabric squares – orange at the bottom, then yellow, then mauve – and pin them behind the design, making sure that the patches extend beyond the marked design in all directions. Tack (baste) in place.

3 Using variegated perlé thread, work big-stitch quilting (a fairly large running stitch, see page 119) around all outlines and along the straight lines of the design.

4 Using small, sharp-pointed scissors, very carefully cut through all the layers of fabric except the bottom orange one, working within the flower petals and centre shape in the channels created by the quilted parallel lines. Use your fingernail to fray all the cut edges gently so that they fluff up.

Smart Stitch

If you plan to do a lot of chenille work, you can buy special scissors and rotary cutters, which will speed up the process.

5 Tack (baste) around the outline of the bag shape (so that the line shows on the back). Trim the coloured fabrics to within this outline if necessary, then put the design right sides together with the second denim square. Stitch round the line, leaving a 10cm (4in) gap along the bottom curve for turning. Trace around the bag outline on to the wrong side of one of the remaining denim squares, then put this one right sides together with the fourth square and stitch round the marked line in the same way.

6 Trim away the excess denim to 6mm (¼in) outside the stitched shape, then clip the curves and corners. Turn each bag panel right side out, push out the corners and slipstitch the openings closed. Put the two sides of the bag right sides together and oversew round the curved edge. Turn the bag right side out.

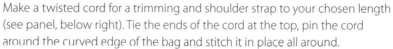

7 Make a twisted cord for a trimming and shoulder strap to your chosen length (see panel, below right). Tie the ends of the cord at the top, pin the cord around the curved edge of the bag and stitch it in place all around.

8 Finish by using matching thread to stitch on buttons or other embellishments.

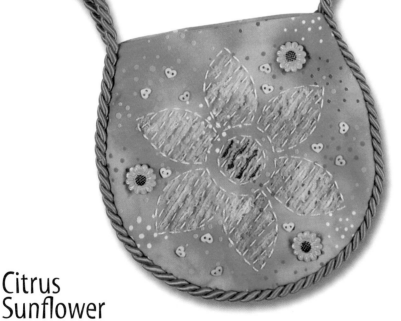

Citrus Sunflower

Make this eye-catching citrus-coloured version of the bag using a sunflower design instead (template on page 103). I added an extra layer of brown fabric behind the centre circle to strengthen the suggestion of a sunflower. Using ready-made cord for the trimming and strap will make sewing even quicker.

(template on page 103)

In a nutshell...

Making cords

Making a twisted cord is simple and useful as it will allow you to match the cord to the fabrics you've used for an attractive co-ordinated look.

1 Cut lengths of assorted threads, three or four times the length of the finished cord required. Knot one end and secure this end to a firm surface using a safety pin.

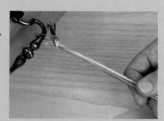

2 Pull the threads out straight and twist them firmly in one direction. Keep twisting until the threads are very tightly twisted.

3 When the threads are twisted tightly and evenly down the length of the cord, bring the two ends together; the cord will twist back on itself, which helps stabilize it. Tie a knot in the other end and use on your project.

Denim Delight template (full size)
*Trace or photocopy the template, cut out the overall
shape and then cut away the daisy petals and flower
centre to create a stencil effect*

Citrus Sunflower template (full size)
*Trace or photocopy the template, cut out the overall
shape and then cut away the sunflower petals and
flower centre to create a stencil effect*

Easter Treats

Whatever treats the Easter Bunny brings you, show them off in this seasonal bonbon basket. The basket is cleverly created from a flat piece of interfacing, covered with bright fabrics and decorated with simple motifs of Easter eggs. If you like, you could add some chicken motifs cut from novelty fabric. The same pattern works well for other celebrations – make it in Christmas prints to hold candy canes and oranges, or try sparkly fabrics for birthday chocolates. I've used pretty butterfly motifs for the basket on page 109.

Easiness Rating ✱✱✱
Techniques Used Using bonding web • Simple machine appliqué
Finished Size The basket is 23cm (9in) square x 7.5cm (3in) high

You will need...

- ✓ 38cm (15in) square of plain yellow cotton fabric
- ✓ 38cm (15in) square and 20cm (8in) square of cotton fabric in a bright print
- ✓ 38cm (15in) square of double-sided Fast2Fuse
- ✓ 20cm (8in) square of double-sided bonding web
- ✓ 1.8m (2yd) pale yellow satin ribbon, 2.5cm (1in) wide
- ✓ Eight flower buttons, beads or fabric shapes
- ✓ Yellow sewing thread
- ✓ Stick glue
- ✓ Soft pencil, long ruler and pale chalk marker
- ✓ Rotary cutter and board (optional)

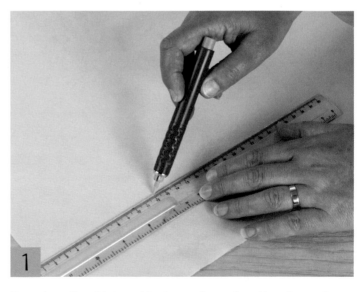

1

Press the yellow fabric and lay it on a flat surface. Use a long ruler and a chalk marker to draw a line 7.5cm (3in) from each edge; this creates four long side sections on the fabric and four square corner pieces. ➤

Follow the bonded appliqué instructions in the panel on page 108 to prepare the small square of bright fabric with bonding web. Trace or photocopy the three egg shapes opposite and cut them out. Use these as templates to draw and cut four eggs of each size from the appliqué fabric. Fuse three shapes on to each side section of the box. As you fuse on the eggs, remember that the outside edge of the fabric will become the top of the box, so make sure that your eggs are the right way up!

Set your machine for a small zigzag and thread it with yellow thread. Go round the edge of each egg shape to appliqué it to the background fabric.

Smart Stitch

Cutting the interfacing as described in step 4, rather than using one whole piece, helps the box to fold crisply at the edges.

On the fusible interfacing, draw a line 7.5cm (3in) from each edge just as you did on the yellow fabric. Cut along these lines to produce one large square, four long rectangles and four small squares. Discard the small squares. Lay the appliquéd design face down on the ironing board and position the sections of interfacing on top. Lay the large square in the centre of the fabric with the rectangles at the sides.

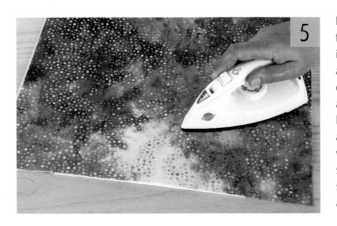

Lay the square of bright fabric on top of the interfacing, right side up and matching the raw edges of the yellow square. Use a warm iron to fuse all the layers together; use an up-and-down pressing motion with the iron rather than sweeping it from side to side, so that the pieces don't move as you are fusing them.

Trim the corners diagonally. Bind the edge of the box by folding the yellow ribbon over it and stitching it in place; fold the ribbon crisply at each corner. Once the whole edge is bound, trim the raw end of the ribbon slightly long then turn it under and stitch it in place to neaten it.

Cut the green ribbon into eight equal lengths and stitch one length to each corner of the octagon shape. Hold the end of the ribbon in place on the outside of the corner with a small dab of stick glue, then stitch a button, charm or fabric flower over the end of the ribbon to ensure that it's securely held.

Tie the ribbons at each corner to create the box shape. If you want to store the box flat after Easter, simply untie the ribbons and flatten the shape again.

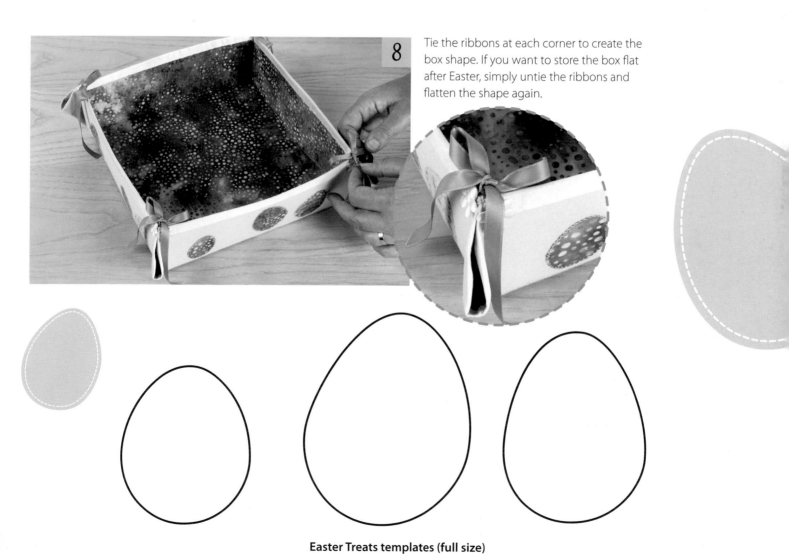

Easter Treats templates (full size)
Trace or photocopy the three egg templates and cut them out. Trace each one four times on to the bonding web

Bonded appliqué

Fusing appliqué shapes into position with double-sided bonding web helps to prevent the edges from fraying, and also keeps the patches in position while you are stitching.

1 Lay the bonding web glue (rough) side down on to the wrong side of your appliqué fabric and fuse it into place with a warm iron.

2 Cut a paper or card template for each different shape and trace the shapes on to the paper (smooth) side of the bonding web.

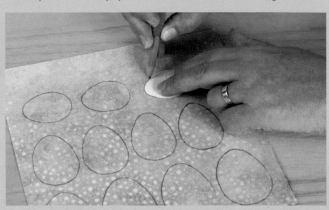

3 Using sharp-pointed scissors, carefully cut out all the shapes, cutting along the marked lines.

4 Peel the backing papers off the shapes, lay them in place on the backing fabric and use a warm iron to fuse the shapes into position.

5 Set your sewing machine for a small zigzag and go round the edge of each shape to appliqué it to the background fabric.

Smart Stitch

Fuse the bonding web on to the fabric *before* you cut out the shapes, to create a good seal around the edges.

Flight of Fancy

Novelty fabrics come printed with all kinds of wonderful motifs; I used a butterfly-print fabric for this variation on the Easter box (right). Fuse bonding web on to the back of the print fabric and cut out the motifs you want to use, then appliqué them as described for the main project. Instead of tying the corners of this box with ribbons, I stitched them together and finished each one with a glittering sequinned butterfly motif in a toning colour.

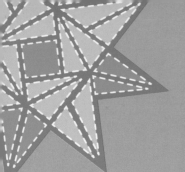

Festive Feasting

A pieced and quilted breadcloth is a wonderful way of keeping freshly baked breads and rolls warm from the oven while you assemble everyone for a Christmas feast. The star design is created in stained-glass patchwork, which makes it simple to stitch – no machine piecing, or matching corners and points! If you prefer, you could use the simpler star design shown on page 115 for your breadcloth or create a colourful set of Christmas table mats.

Easiness Rating ✱✱✱
Techniques Used Stained-glass patchwork • Simple hand embroidery
Finished Size 50cm (20in) square

You will need...

✓ Eight different Christmas-print fabrics (see diagram page 113 for which fabric goes where, to choose a suitable mix of colours and tones):
  - 8cm (3in) of fabric A
  - 15cm (6in) square of fabric B
  - 20cm (8in) squares of fabric C, D, E and F
  - 30cm (12in) square of fabric G
  - 50cm (20in) square of background fabric H

✓ 50cm (20in) square of compressed wadding (batting)

✓ 50cm (20in) square of backing fabric

✓ 6m (7yd) red satin ribbon, 9mm (³⁄₈in) wide

✓ 2m (2yd) red satin ribbon, 3.5cm (1½in) wide

✓ Red sewing thread

✓ Coton à broder in red or green for embroidery

1

Trace or photocopy the templates on page 114 and cut them out. Use template 1 to cut four patches from fabric D and four from fabric F. Use template 2 to cut four patches from fabric G, and then use template 3 to cut four patches from fabric E. Remember to use the templates right side up on the right side of the fabrics. ➤

Fold the square of background fabric in half vertically, then fold it again into quarters and press the folded edges. These folds will help you when you are positioning the fabric patches. Unfold the square and lay it right side up on a flat surface. Position the square of fabric C on top, right side up, in the middle, using the folds to help you position it centrally (each corner of the square will lie on a fold line). Pin the square in place.

Position the square of fabric B on top as shown, with each corner touching one edge of the fabric C square. Finally, pin the square of fabric A in the exact centre of the design.

Pin the triangles of fabrics D and E in position, using the layout diagram opposite as a guide to remind you where each one goes. You will find that the patches overlap each other slightly; this helps to keep them in place while you're stitching. Secure the patches in position with a medium-width machine zigzag, and add lines of stitching to mark the straight lines around the small central square, as shown on the diagram.

Cover each of the joins between the patches with a length of narrow ribbon, stitching the ribbon in place by machine. Make sure that you tuck the raw ends of the ribbon strips underneath other strips where two meet. If you prefer, you can use fancy stitches on your machine to attach the ribbon strips, as I've done.

Draw a diagonal line across each corner of the design and trim the corners of the background square away to make an octagon. Cut the squares of backing fabric and wadding to the same shape.

Smart Stitch

Before attaching the wide ribbon, spray with starch, fold in half lengthways and press dry. This makes it easier to work with, and the fold helps position it over the raw cloth edge.

Lay the backing fabric on a flat surface, right side down, and cover it with the wadding, matching the raw edges. Lay the star design on top, right side up, and pin the layers together. Bind the edges with the wider ribbon, pinning it in place first and slipstitching the edges on the front and back of the work. Fold the ribbon crisply at each corner of the octagon.

Use the red and green threads to work seeding stitches (see page 118) on the breadcloth to quilt and decorate it.

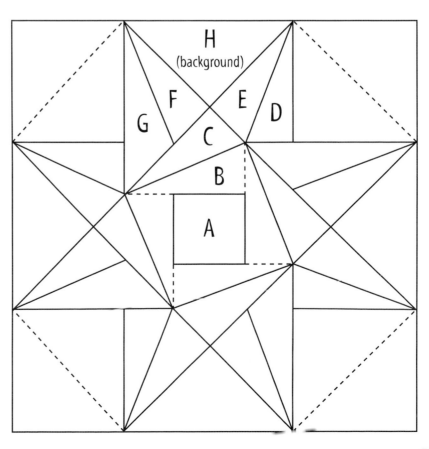

Festive Feasting layout diagram
Use this diagram to help you position the fabric shapes in the correct places

Festive Feasting templates (full size)
Trace or photocopy the shapes and cut them out.
Use template 1 to cut four shapes from fabric D and
four from fabric F; use template 2 to cut four shapes
from fabric G, and template 3 to cut four shapes
from fabric E

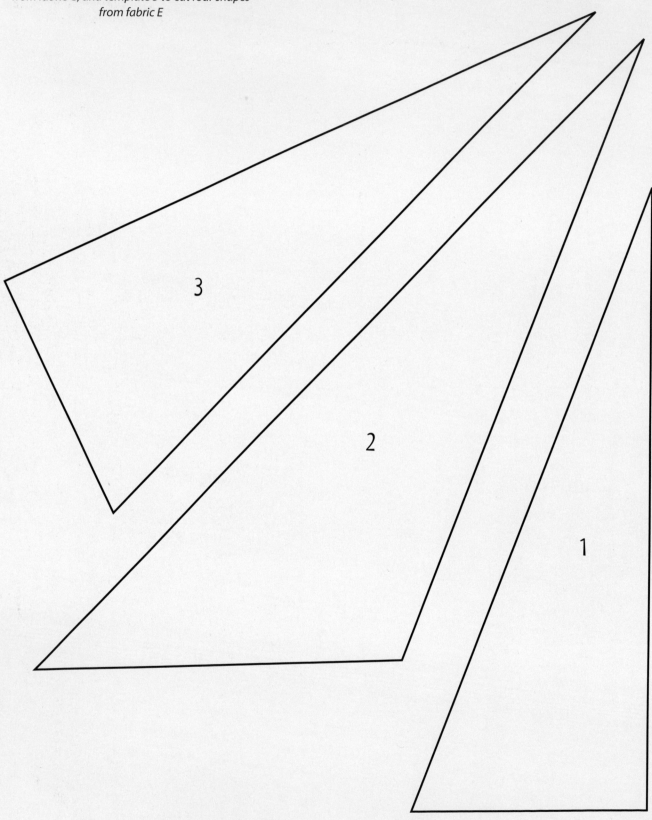

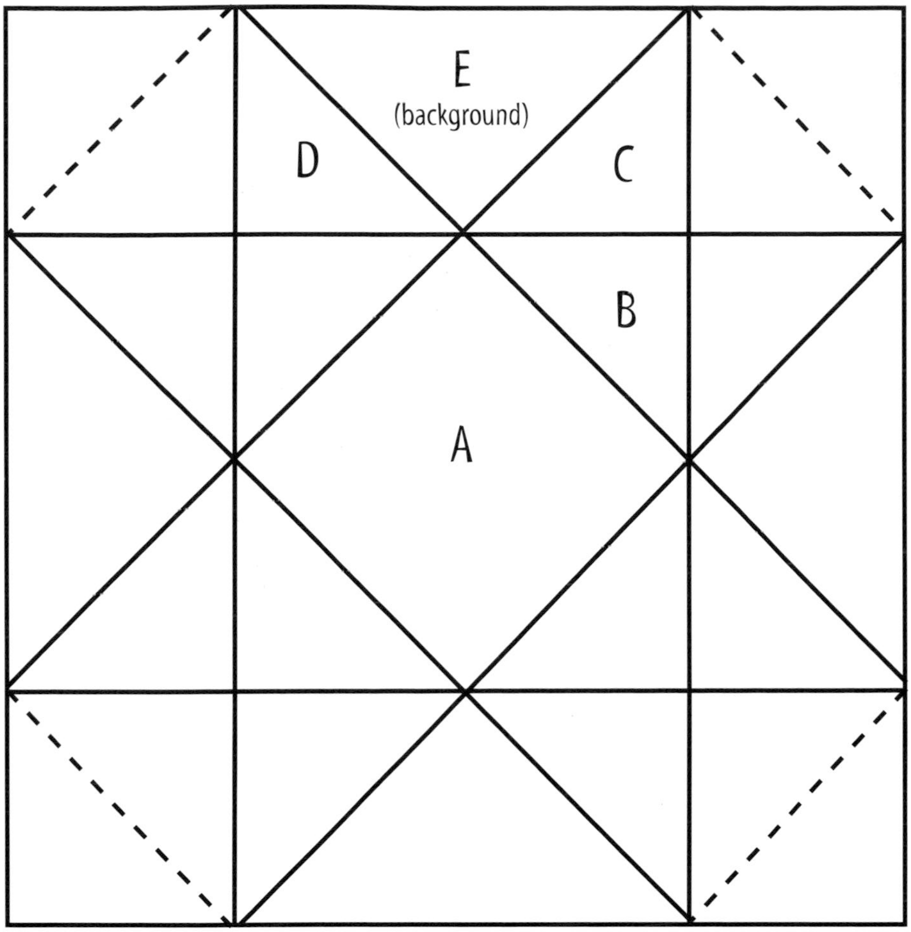

Simple Star design
Draw a square at the finished size you require. Divide it into a 4 x 4 grid and then copy the lines of the design into the grid. Cut out the relevant patches and use them as templates for your fabric patches

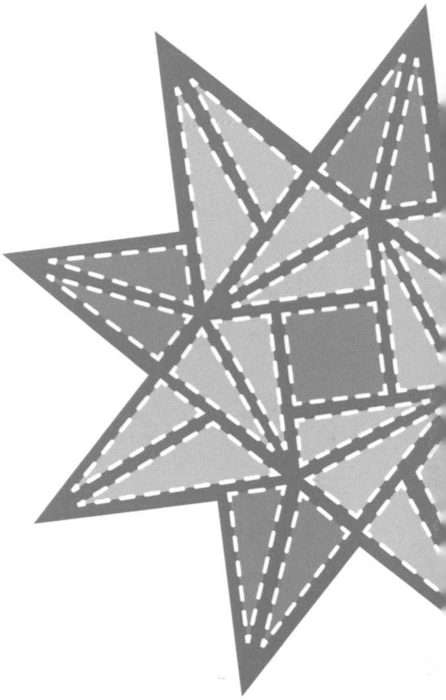

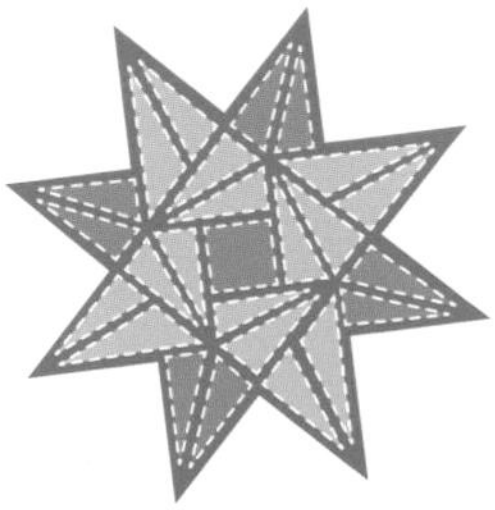

Simple Star

This simple star design can be used to make a breadcloth in the same way as the main project – or why not make several at a smaller size as table mats to complement the breadcloth? The design is based on a simple 4 x 4 grid, so draw it up at the size you want and use the shapes as templates. Use one large square of fabric B, behind the diamond of fabric A, and cut four triangles from template C and four from template D. Fabric E is the large background square.

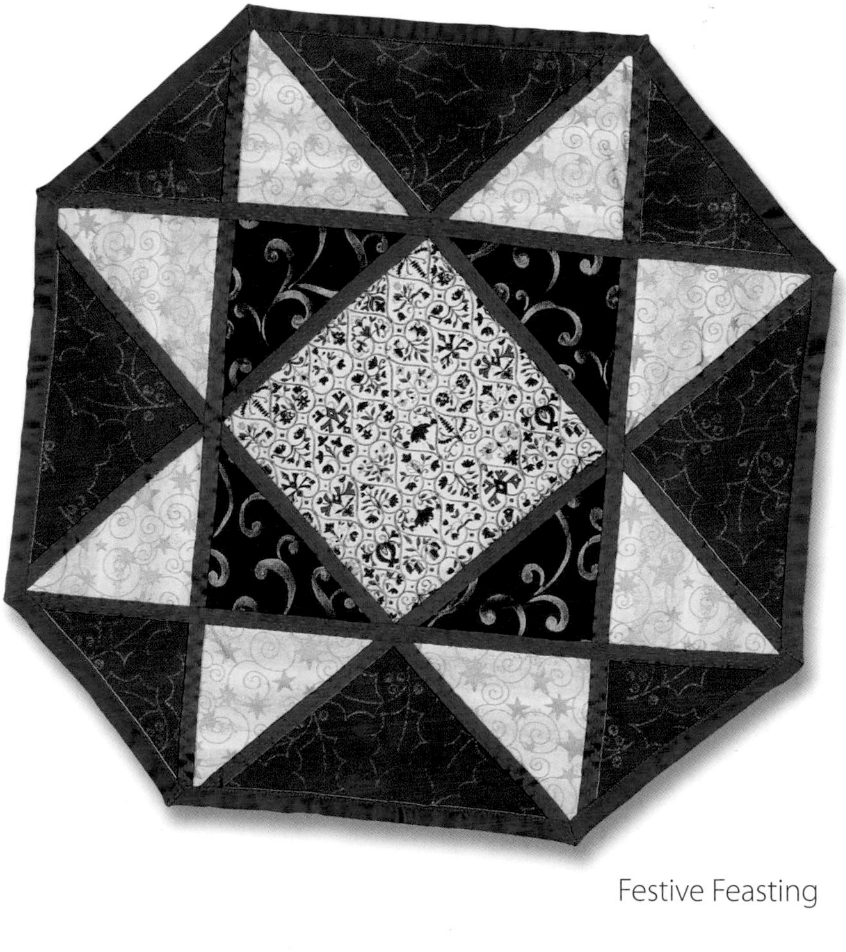

Useful Stitches

The projects use a variety of stitches for functional and decorative work but they are all basic stitches that are very easy to work. Follow the sequenced diagrams given here. See overleaf for advice on quilting.

Backstitch

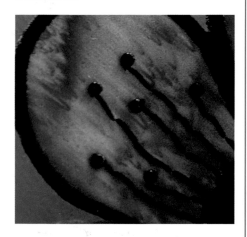

Backstitch is used to create a medium-weight stitched line. It also works well for creating the channels in Italian/corded quilting (see page 72). To work backstitch, follow the diagram below: bring the needle out at the beginning of the stitching line, take a medium-length straight stitch and bring the needle out slightly further along the stitching line (a). Insert the needle at the end of the first stitch and bring it out slightly further still along the stitching line (b). Continue in the same way to create a line of joined stitches.

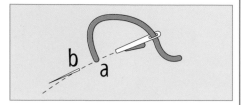

Blanket Stitch

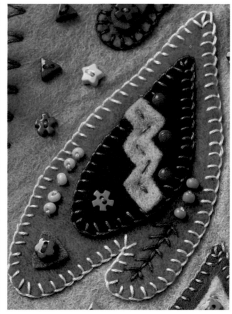

This is a very versatile stitch that is also called buttonhole stitch when worked closely together as an edging stitch. It can also be worked as an outline, as a circle or as closed buttonhole stitch (see the needlebook on page 20). Follow the sequence in the diagram below.

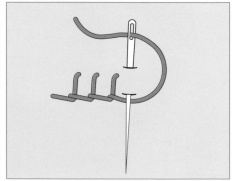

Feather Stitch

Feather stitch is a very old stitch that can be used for outlines, for borders or fillings or to decorate hems. The stitches are worked from top to bottom – follow the sequence in the diagrams below.

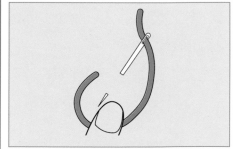

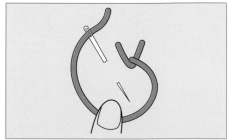

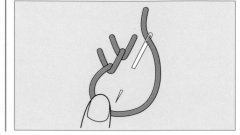

Fern Stitch

Fern stitch is formed from groups of three straight stitches, worked so they create a fan shape. Follow the diagram, beginning with a central stitch (a), followed by a diagonal stitch to each side (b and c). Work the next central straight stitch so that it joins the end of the previous one.

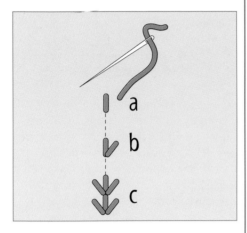

Herringbone Stitch

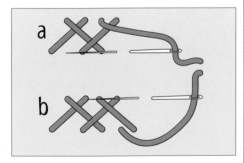

This is another highly versatile stitch. Following the diagrams, work from left to right along the stitching line. Make a small stitch from right to left below the stitching line (a), then follow this with a similar stitch above the stitching line (b). If you are left-handed, work the stitch from right to left along the stitching line.

Ladder Stitch

This is a very useful stitch for closing gaps in stuffed items such as pincushions and herb cushions as it is generally worked between two folded edges. Take straight stitches into the folded fabric, stitching into each edge in turn. After a few stitches, pull the thread taut to draw up the stitches and close the gap.

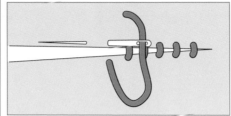

Machine Satin Stitch

Machine satin stitch is used in many of the projects to appliqué fabric patches and also to provide a decorative effect. If the project is using a foundation paper, begin by positioning this under the work and then stitch an even satin stitch along each line of the design. Work as fast as you feel comfortable and can safely do while still being in good control of your machine – the faster you can stitch, the more even the satin stitch will be.

If the end of the line of satin stitch will be covered by a subsequent line you don't need to finish it off neatly but just stop stitching and neaten the end of the first line with the later line of stitching. If it won't be covered by a later line, move the stitch width to zero

and work a couple of stitches in place if you want the line to end with a straight edge.

If you want the line to taper, slowly reduce the width of the stitch as you near the end of the line, until you finish with it at zero at the end of the line. Don't work reverse stitches over the line of satin stitch to finish them as this will look too bulky. When all stitching is finished, remove the foundation paper.

You can create some beautiful effects with simple machine satin stitch, as I did with the picture frame on page 49. Curving lines of satin stitch also lend themselves well to bead embellishment, as you can see by the stitching detail below.

Running Stitch

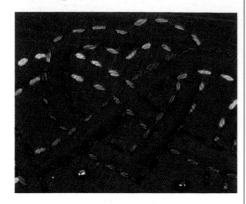

This is the most straightforward of the embroidery stitches. It is useful for creating the channels in Italian/corded quilting (see page 72) and a variation of it is used for hand quilting (see big-stitch quilting, opposite). To work running stitch, bring the needle out on the front of the work and take a series of small, even stitches along the stitching line. If you put the needle in and out of the fabric several times before pulling the thread through, it helps to keep stitches even and create a smooth line.

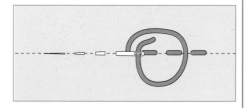

Seeding Stitches

Seeding is simply a random arrangement of short stitches (see diagram below). These are often used as a filling or to suggest texture. The stitches can be any length, from tiny dots to quite long straight stitches.

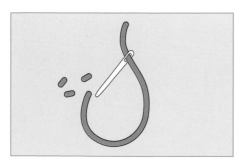

Slipstitch

Slipstitch is a versatile stitch that can be used for hand appliqué and for tasks such as catching down bindings and casings. Take the needle into the background fabric, as close to the top fabric as possible, then bring it out at a slant so that it emerges just on the turned edge of the top fabric. As you pull the stitches taut they will virtually disappear under the top fabric.

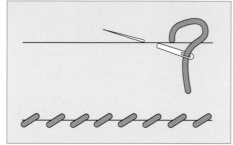

Whipped Running Stitch

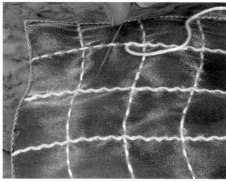

Following the diagrams, work a line of even, medium-length running stitches through the fabric (a). Thread a bodkin or tapestry needle with a second thread, then slip the needle under each running stitch (b), taking the needle under the stitch in the same direction each time.

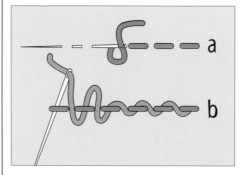

Quilting

Quilting is a straightforward technique of working tiny running stitches along the lines of a design. The stitching is usually worked on a quilt 'sandwich', drawing the layers of front, batting and back together to create a puffed texture. Quilting can be done by hand or machine, or by a combination of the two.

Hand Quilting

Hand quilting is best worked in specialized quilting thread as this is stronger than normal sewing thread and is robust enough to withstand being pulled through the fabric numerous times without snapping or tangling. It's also possible to do hand quilting using fine silk threads and some metallic threads.

Thread your needle with a length of quilting thread and tie a knot in the end. Bring the needle out on the front of the work, pulling gently until the knot pops through the fabric and hides itself in the wadding (batting). Working with a rocking motion, take the needle in and out of the fabric several times along the stitching line (see a in the diagram below), then pull the thread through to create a row of small, even running stitches (b). The number of stitches per inch or centimetre isn't as important as making them even in length; uneven stitches create a rather untidy appearance. When you've finished the line of stitching, or need a new length of thread, make a knot in the thread just beyond your last stitch (c) and pull it through the fabric so that it too is hidden in the wadding (batting).

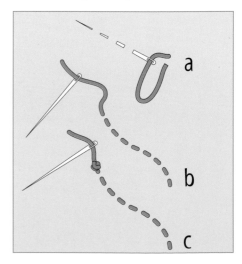

I used a type of hand quilting called big-stitch quilting on the denim bag on page 99 (see photos right). Here, the stitches are large and create a decorative effect on the front of the work, as well as doing the task of quilting a design into the fabric layers. The stitches are often worked in a colour that contrasts with the background fabric.

To work this kind of quilting, take quite long, even running stitches along the line of the design, making each stitch roughly twice as long on the front of the work as it is on the back (see a in the diagram below). Take several stitches on the needle at the same time as this will make the stitches more even and keep the lines of stitching accurate. At points and corners, you can either work the stitches so there's a small gap at the angle (b), or so that the two meet exactly at the angle (c). Try not to mix the two in the same project, or the design will look uneven.

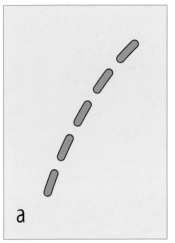
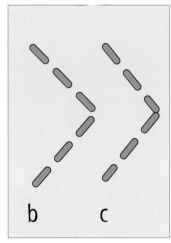

a   b   c

Machine Quilting

There are many ways in which quilting can be done by sewing machine, and the method used will depend on the finished effect you're looking for. I used simple straight line machine quilting on the wedding ring cushion on page 29 to create a trellis pattern around the lace-filled heart.

The simplest kind of machine quilting consists of lines of straight machine stitching; these can be worked in a regular design (see a in the diagram below) or an irregular one (b). If your machine does fancy stitches, you can also use these in various ways to create lines, little patches or shapes on the quilt sandwich. Some of the stitches can also be used to appliqué cord or decorative threads on to the fabric, quilting and embellishing at the same time.

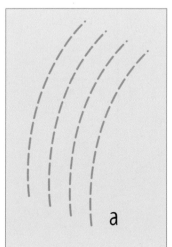
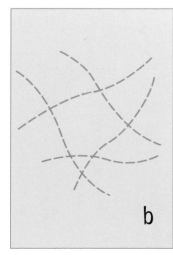

a   b

Suppliers

There are, of course, many shops that stock patchwork supplies; these are some of the ones I use most often.

The Bramble Patch
West Street, Weedon, Northants NN7 4QU, UK
tel: 01327 342212
www.thebramblepatch.co.uk
For patchwork fabrics and threads

The Button Lady
16 Hollyfield Road, South Sutton Coldfield,
West Midlands, B76 1NX, UK
tel: 0121 3293234
For buttons and charms

Gregory Knopp
PO Box 158, Gillingham, Kent, ME7 3HF, UK
www.gregory-knopp.co.uk
For every kind of button and embellishment

Hancock's of Paducah
3841 Hinkleville, Paducah KY 42001, USA
email:
customerservice@hancocks-paducah.com
www.hancocks-paducah.com
For fabrics

Kaleidoscope
5 Pendicle Road, Bearsden, Glasgow
G61 1PU, Scotland
tel: 0141 9428511
email: customer.care@kalquilts.com
www.kalquilts.com
*For patchwork fabrics and quilting books;
stockists of Fast2Fuse*

Kreinik Manufacturing Company Inc
3106 Timanus Lane, Suite 101, Baltimore,
MD 21244 USA
tel: 1800 537 2166
email: kreinik@kreinik.com
www.kreinik.com
For a wide range of metallic threads

Lords Sew-Knit Centre
Oswaldtwistle Mills, Colliers Street,
Oswaldtwistle, Accrington, Lancs BB5 3DE, UK
tel: 01254 389171
www.lordsewing.co.uk
Stockists of Fast2Fuse and other stabilizers

Madeira (USA) Ltd
PO Box 6068, 30 Bayside Court, Laconia,
NH03246, USA
tel: 603 528 4264
For Madeira threads

The Silk Route
Cross Cottage, Cross Lane, Frimley Green,
Surrey, GU16 6LN, UK
tel: 01252 835781
www.thesilkroute.co.uk
For all kinds of silk fabrics and threads

Acknowledgments
Thanks to:
Lin, Ame, Pru and Cheryl of David & Charles, for all their hard work in producing this book.
All the workshop students who keep demanding new projects, and so keep my work and ideas fresh!
Rachel McIntyre, for her excellent stitching on Funky Felt and Heart to Heart.
Karl, for his patience and technical expertise over the photography.
Chris, the other half of Teamwork.

About the Author
Gail Lawther is a quilter, author and teacher who has written many books on different aspects of quilting and needlecraft. Her unique pieces have won numerous awards at quilt fairs and competitions; she is particularly known for her work in stained glass patchwork, and her commissioned work includes various sets of church banners using this technique. Gail can be contacted at:

44 Rectory Walk, Sompting, Lancing, West Sussex BN15 0DU
email: thelawthers@ntlworld.com
www.gail-quilts-plus.co.uk

Index